Year 7, Pupil Book 3

NEW MATHS FRAMEWORKING

Matches the revised KS3 Framework

Kevin Evans, Keith Gordon, Trevor Senior, Brian Speed

Contents

Introduction

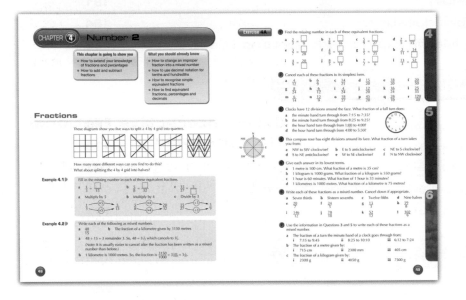

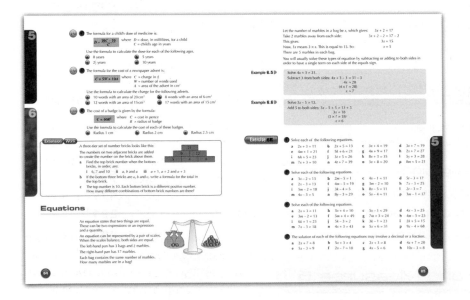

Learning objectives

See what you are going to cover and what you should already know at the start of each chapter. The purple and blue boxes set the topic in context and provide a handy checklist.

National Curriculum levels

Know what level you are working at so you can easily track your progress with the colour-coded levels at the side of the page.

Worked examples

Understand the topic before you start the exercises by reading the examples in blue boxes. These take you through how to answer a question step-by-step.

Functional Maths

Practise your Functional Maths skills to see how people use Maths in everyday life.

Look out for the Functional Maths icon on the page.

Extension activities

Stretch your thinking and investigative skills by working through the extension activities. By tackling these you are working at a higher level.

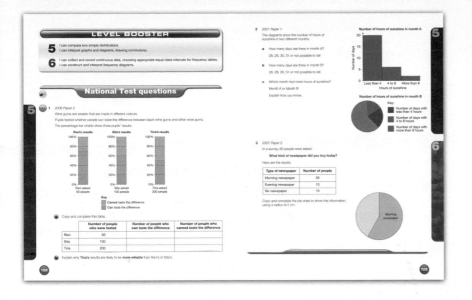

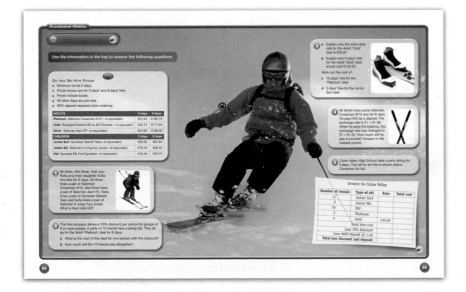

Level booster

Progress to the next level by checking the Level boosters at the end of each chapter. These clearly show you what you need to know at each level and how to improve.

National Test questions

Practise the past paper Test questions to feel confident and prepared for your KS3 National Curriculum Tests. The questions are levelled so you can check what level you are working at.

Extra interactive National Test practice

Watch and listen to the audio/visual National Test questions on the separate Interactive Book CD-ROM to help you revise as a class on a whiteboard.

 Look out for the computer mouse icon on the page and on the screen.

Functional Maths activities

Put Maths into context with these colourful pages showing real-world situations involving Maths. You are practising your Functional Maths skills by analysing data to solve problems.

Extra interactive Functional Maths questions and video clips

Extend your Functional Maths skills by taking part in the interactive questions on the separate Interactive Book CD-ROM. Your teacher can put these on the whiteboard so the class can answer the questions on the board.

See Maths in action by watching the video clips and doing the related Worksheets on the Interactive Book CD-ROM. The videos bring the Functional Maths activities to life and help you see how Maths is used in the real world.

Look out for the computer mouse icon on the page and on the screen.

This chapter is going to show you

- Some simple number patterns that you may have seen before, and how to describe them
- How to create sequences and describe them in words
- How to generate and describe simple whole-number sequences

What you should already know

- Odd and even numbers
- Times tables up to 10×10

Sequences and rules

You can make up many different sequences with integers (whole numbers) using simple rules.

Example **1.1**

Rule: add 3   Starting at 1 gives the sequence 1, 4, 7, 10, 13, …

                               Starting at 6 gives the sequence 6, 9, 12, 15, 18, …

Rule: double   Starting at 1 gives the sequence 1, 2, 4, 8, 16, …

                               Starting at 5 gives the sequence 5, 10, 20, 40, 80, …

So you see, with *different* **rules** and *different* **starting points**, there are very many *different* **sequences** you may make.

The numbers in a sequence are called **terms** and the starting point is called the **1st term**. The rule is often referred to as the **term-to-term rule**.

Exercise **1A**

1 Use each of the following term-to-term rules with the 1st terms **i** 1 and **ii** 5. Create each sequence with five terms in it.

   a   add 9   **b**   multiply by 5   **c**   add 7   **d**   multiply by 9

2 Give the next two terms in each of these sequences. Describe the term-to-term rule you have used.

   a   2, 4, 6, …   **b**   3, 6, 9, …   **c**   1, 10, 100, …   **d**   1, 2, 4, …

   e   2, 10, 50, …   **f**   0, 7, 14, …   **g**   7, 10, 13, …   **h**   2, 6, 18, …

4

3 Give the next two terms in these sequences. Describe the term-to-term rule you have used.

    a   50, 45, 40, 35, 30, …   **b**   35, 32, 29, 26, 23, …

    c   64, 32, 16, 8, 4, …   **d**   3125, 625, 125, 25, 5, …

    e   20, 19.3, 18.6, 17.9, 17.2, …   **f**   1000, 100, 10, 1, 0.1, …

    g   10, 7, 4, 1, −2, …   **h**   27, 9, 3, 1, $\frac{1}{3}$, …

4 For each pair of numbers find at least two different sequences, writing the next two terms. Describe the term-to-term rule you have used.

    a   1, 4, …   **b**   3, 7, …   **c**   2, 6, …

    d   3, 6, …   **e**   4, 8, …   **f**   5, 15, …

5 Find two terms between each pair of numbers to form a sequence. Describe the term-to-term rule you have used.

    a   1, …, …, 8   **b**   3, …, …, 12   **c**   5, …, …, 20

    d   4, …, …, 10   **e**   80, …, …, 10   **f**   2, …, …, 54

Extension Work

1   **i**   Make up some of your own sequences and describe them.

      ii Give your sequences to someone else and see if they can find out what your term-to-term rule is.

2   Use a spreadsheet or graphics calculator for this investigation.

    Here is an incomplete rule to find the next term in a sequence:

    Add on ☐

    Find a 1st term for the sequence and a number to go in the box so that all the terms in the sequence are:

    a   odd   **b**   even   **c**   multiples of 5   **d**   numbers ending in 7

Finding missing terms

In any sequence, you will have a 1st term, 2nd term, 3rd term, 4th term and so on.

Example 1.2 ▶

In the sequence 3, 5, 7, 9, …, what is the 5th term, and what is the 50th term?

You first need to know what the term-to-term rule is. You can see that you add 2 from one term to the next:

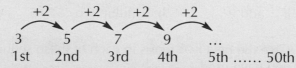

To get to the 5th term, you add 2 to the 4th term, which gives 11.

To get to the 50th term, you will have to add on 2 a total of 49 times (50 − 1) to the first term, 3. This will give $3 + 2 \times 49 = 3 + 98 = 101$.

Exercise 1B

1 In each of the following sequences, find the 5th and the 50th term.

a   4, 6, 8, 10, …   b   1, 6, 11, 16, …   c   3, 10, 17, 24, …
d   5, 8, 11, 14, …   e   1, 5, 9, 13, …   f   2, 10, 18, 26, …
g   20, 30, 40, 50, …   h   10, 19, 28, 37, …   i   3, 9, 15, 21, …

2 In each of the sequences below, find the 1st term, then find the 50th term.

In each case, you have been given the 4th, 5th and 6th terms.

a   …, …, …, 13, 15, 17, …   b   …, …, …, 18, 23, 28, …
c   …, …, …, 19, 23, 27, …   d   …, …, …, 32, 41, 50, …

3 In each of the following sequences, find the missing terms and the 50th term.

Term	1st	2nd	3rd	4th	5th	6th	7th	8th	50th
Sequence A	…	…	…	…	17	19	21	23	…
Sequence B	…	9	…	19	…	29	…	39	…
Sequence C	…	…	16	23	…	37	44	…	…
Sequence D	…	…	25	…	45	…	…	75	…
Sequence E	…	5	…	11	…	…	20	…	…
Sequence F	…	…	12	…	…	18	…	22	…

4 Find the 40th term in the sequence with the term-to-term rule ADD 5 and a 1st term of 6.

5 Find the 80th term in the sequence with the term-to-term rule ADD 4 and a 1st term of 9.

6 Find the 100th term in the sequence with the term-to-term rule ADD 7 and 1st term of 1.

7 Find the 30th term in the sequence with the term-to-term rule ADD 11 and 1st term of 5.

Extension **Work**

1 You have a simple sequence where the 50th term is 349, the 51st is 354 and the 52nd is 359. Find the 1st term and the 100th term.

2 You are building patterns using black and yellow squares.

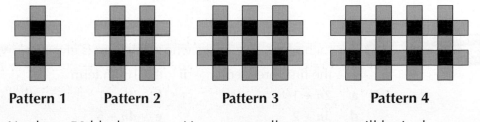

Pattern 1   Pattern 2   Pattern 3   Pattern 4

You have 50 black squares. How many yellow squares will be in the pattern?

Finding the general term (*n*th term)

We can describe a sequence by finding the **nth term**. This is the **generalisation** that will allow us to find any specific term we want.

Example 1.3 ▶

The *n*th term of the sequence 8, 13, 18, 23, 28, … is given by the expression $5n + 3$.

a Show this is true for the first three terms.

b Use the rule to find the 50th term of the sequence.

a Let $n = 1$, $5 \times 1 + 3 = 5 + 3 = 8$
Let $n = 2$, $5 \times 2 + 3 = 10 + 3 = 13$
Let $n = 3$, $5 \times 3 + 3 = 15 + 3 = 18$

b Let $n = 50$, $5 \times 50 + 3 = 250 + 3 = 253$
so the 50th term is 253.

Example 1.4 ▶

Look at the sequence with the following pattern.

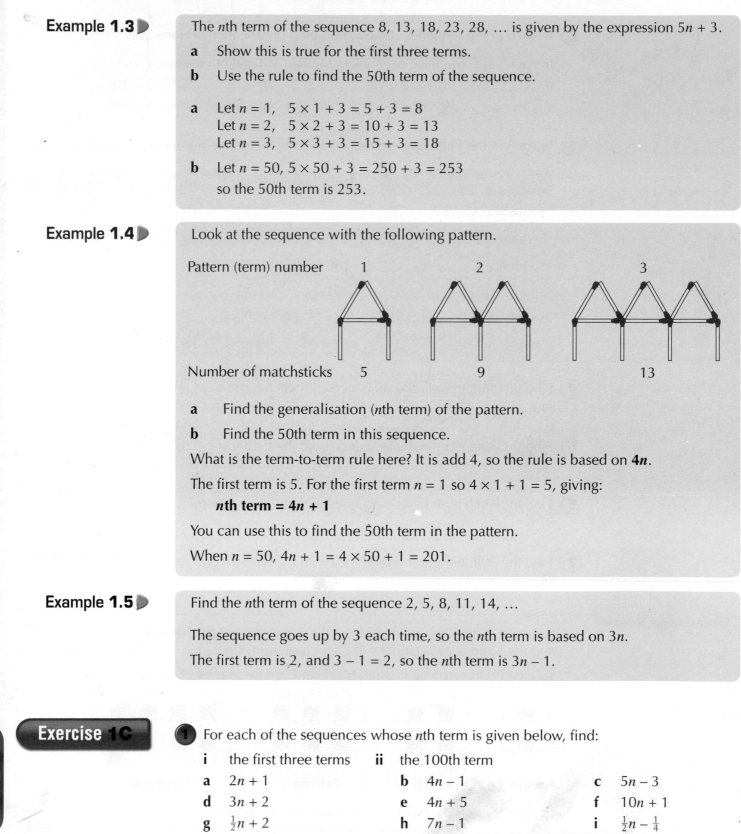

Pattern (term) number   1   2   3

Number of matchsticks   5   9   13

a Find the generalisation (*n*th term) of the pattern.

b Find the 50th term in this sequence.

What is the term-to-term rule here? It is add 4, so the rule is based on **4*n***.

The first term is 5. For the first term $n = 1$ so $4 \times 1 + 1 = 5$, giving:

nth term = 4n + 1

You can use this to find the 50th term in the pattern.

When $n = 50$, $4n + 1 = 4 \times 50 + 1 = 201$.

Example 1.5 ▶

Find the *n*th term of the sequence 2, 5, 8, 11, 14, …

The sequence goes up by 3 each time, so the *n*th term is based on 3*n*.

The first term is 2, and $3 - 1 = 2$, so the *n*th term is $3n - 1$.

Exercise 1C

① For each of the sequences whose *n*th term is given below, find:

i the first three terms   **ii** the 100th term

a $2n + 1$ **b** $4n - 1$ **c** $5n - 3$

d $3n + 2$ **e** $4n + 5$ **f** $10n + 1$

g $\frac{1}{2}n + 2$ **h** $7n - 1$ **i** $\frac{1}{2}n - \frac{1}{4}$

2 For each of the patterns below, find:

   i   the *n*th term for the number of matchsticks

   ii   the number of matchsticks in the 50th term

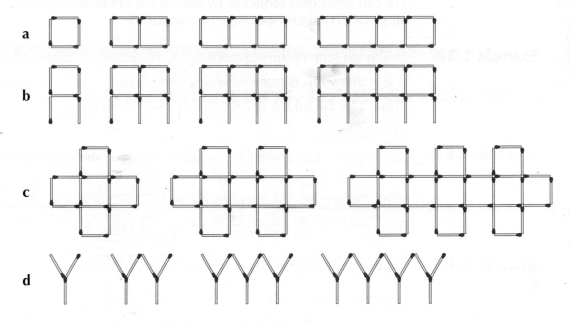

   a

   b

   c

   d

3 Find the *n*th term of each of the following sequences.

   a   3, 9, 15, 21, 27, …   **b**   10, 13, 16, 19, 22, …

   c   7, 13, 19, 25, 31, …   **d**   1, 4, 7, 10, 13, …

   e   4, 11, 18, 25, 32, …   **f**   5, 7, 9, 11, 13, …

   g   9, 13, 17, 21, 25, …   **h**   5, 13, 21, 29, 37, …

   i   11, 21, 31, 41, 51, …   **j**   3, 12, 21, 30, 39, …

4 The patterns below contain two different colours of matchsticks. Find the *n*th term for:

   i   the number of red-tipped matchsticks   **ii** the number of blue-tipped matchsticks

   iii   the total number of matchsticks

Use your generalisations to describe the 50th term in the patterns by finding:

   iv   the number of red-tipped matchsticks   **v** the number of blue-tipped matchsticks

   vi   the total number of matchsticks

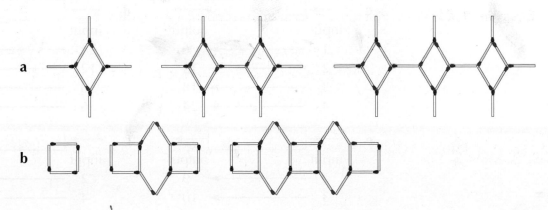

   a

   b

For each of the sequences below whose nth term is given, find:

i the first three terms   **ii** the 100th term

a n^2 **b** $(n + 2)(n + 1)$ **c** $\frac{1}{2}n(n + 1)$

Functions and mappings

Example 1.6 ▷

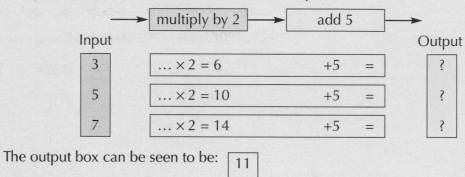

Complete the function machine to show the output.

multiply by 2 ⟶ add 5

Input		Output
3	... × 2 = 6 +5 =	?
5	... × 2 = 10 +5 =	?
7	... × 2 = 14 +5 =	?

The output box can be seen to be:

11

15

19

Exercise 1D

1 Express each of these functions in words.

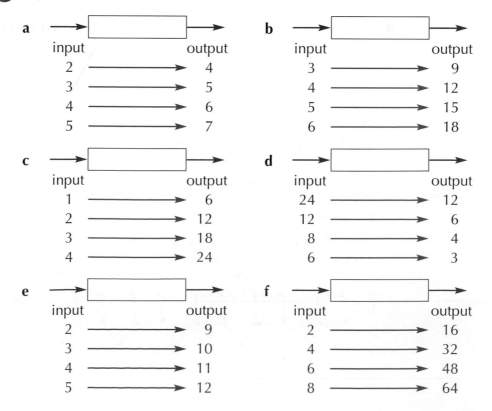

a

input	output
2	4
3	5
4	6
5	7

b

input	output
3	9
4	12
5	15
6	18

c

input	output
1	6
2	12
3	18
4	24

d

input	output
24	12
12	6
8	4
6	3

e

input	output
2	9
3	10
4	11
5	12

f

input	output
2	16
4	32
6	48
8	64

2 Find the missing values in these double function machines.

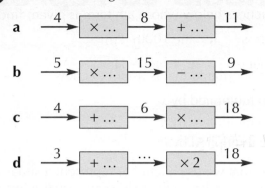

a $\xrightarrow{4}$ [× ...] $\xrightarrow{8}$ [+ ...] $\xrightarrow{11}$

b $\xrightarrow{5}$ [× ...] $\xrightarrow{15}$ [− ...] $\xrightarrow{9}$

c $\xrightarrow{4}$ [+ ...] $\xrightarrow{6}$ [× ...] $\xrightarrow{18}$

d $\xrightarrow{3}$ [+ ...] $\xrightarrow{...}$ [× 2] $\xrightarrow{18}$

3 Each of the following functions is made up from two operations, as above.
Find the **combined functions** in each case.

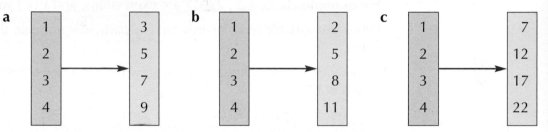

a

1	3
2	5
3	7
4	9

b

1	2
2	5
3	8
4	11

c

1	7
2	12
3	17
4	22

4 Work backwards from each output to find the input to each of the following functions.

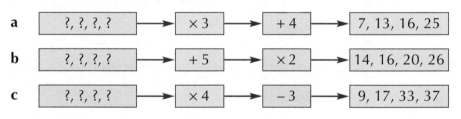

a [?, ?, ?, ?] ⟶ [× 3] ⟶ [+ 4] ⟶ [7, 13, 16, 25]

b [?, ?, ?, ?] ⟶ [+ 5] ⟶ [× 2] ⟶ [14, 16, 20, 26]

c [?, ?, ?, ?] ⟶ [× 4] ⟶ [− 3] ⟶ [9, 17, 33, 37]

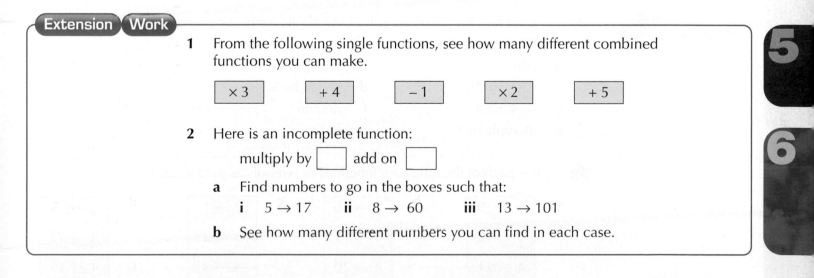

Extension Work

1 From the following single functions, see how many different combined functions you can make.

[× 3]   [+ 4]   [− 1]   [× 2]   [+ 5]

2 Here is an incomplete function:

multiply by ☐ add on ☐

a Find numbers to go in the boxes such that:

   i 5 → 17   **ii** 8 → 60   **iii** 13 → 101

b See how many different numbers you can find in each case.

Using letter symbols to represent functions

Here is some algebra shorthand that is useful to know:

$2x$ means two multiplied by x

$2g$ means two multiplied by g

$5h$ means five multiplied by h

The idea of algebra is that we use a letter to represent a situation where we do not know a number (value) or where we know the value can vary (be lots of different numbers).

Each of the above is an **expression**. An expression is often a mixture of letters, numbers and signs. We call the letters **variables**, because the values they stand for vary.

For example, $3x$, $x + 5$, $2x + 7$ are expressions, and x is a variable in each case.

When the variable in an expression is a particular number, the expression has a particular value.

For example, in the expression $x + 6$, when $x = 4$, the expression has the value $4 + 6$, which is 10.

Example 1.7 ▶

Draw mapping diagrams to illustrate each of the following functions.

a $x \rightarrow x + 5$ **b** $x \rightarrow 3x$ **c** $x \rightarrow 2x + 1$

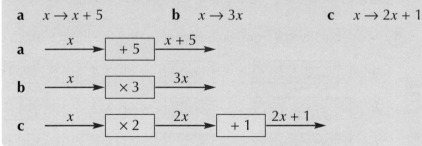

Exercise 1E

①   Write each of the following rules in symbolic form. For example, add 4 can be written as $x \rightarrow x + 4$.

a   add 3   **b**   multiply by 5

c   subtract 2   **d**   divide by 5

e   subtract 4   **f**   double

g   multiply by 8   **h**   halve

②   Express each of the following functions in symbols as in Question 1.

a

$2 \rightarrow 9$
$3 \rightarrow 10$
$4 \rightarrow 11$
$5 \rightarrow 12$

b

$2 \rightarrow 10$
$3 \rightarrow 15$
$4 \rightarrow 20$
$5 \rightarrow 25$

c

$2 \rightarrow 1$
$3 \rightarrow 2$
$4 \rightarrow 3$
$5 \rightarrow 4$

d

$2 \rightarrow 8$
$3 \rightarrow 12$
$4 \rightarrow 16$
$5 \rightarrow 20$

Draw mapping diagrams to illustrate each of these functions.

    a $x \rightarrow 2x + 3$

    b $x \rightarrow 3x - 2$

    c $x \rightarrow 5x + 1$

    d $x \rightarrow 10x - 3$

4 Describe each of the following mappings as functions in the symbolic form, as above.

a

1 → 1
2 → 3
3 → 5
4 → 7

b

1 → 7
2 → 11
3 → 15
4 → 19

c

1 → 1
2 → 4
3 → 7
4 → 10

d

1 → 11
2 → 21
3 → 31
4 → 41

5 Put the same number through each of these function machines.

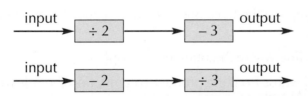

Repeat with other numbers.

Can you find an input that gives the same output for both function machines?

6 Put the same number through each of these function machines.

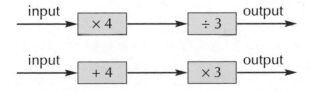

Repeat with other numbers.

Can you find an input that gives the same output for both function machines?

7 The diagram shows a number machine.

Input ➝ × 5 ➝ − 40 ➝ Output

    a   Write down the output when the input is 8.

    b   Find a number to input, so that the output is the same as the input.

Extension **Work**

Think about a group of people who meet and want to shake each other's hands.

One person alone would have no one to shake hands with.

Two people would shake hands just once.

Three people would have three handshakes altogether.

Four people would have six handshakes altogether.

Put these results into the following table.

Number of people	Number of handshakes	Two times number of handshakes	Product
1	0	0	0×1
2	1	2	1×2
3	3	6	2×3
4			

Copy and complete the table and extend it to give the number of handshakes for 10 people.

Finally add a line where the number of people is n.

Working backwards from the product column, find the rule for the number of handshakes when there are n people.

A function investigation

Activity **Work**

Every two-digit whole number can be written as $10a + b$.

For example, $28 = 10 \times 2 + 8$.

Consider the function $\boxed{10x + y \rightarrow 10y - x}$

$$36 \rightarrow 60 - 3 = 57$$
$$19 \rightarrow 90 - 1 = 89$$
$$75 \rightarrow 50 - 7 = 43$$

1 Start with any two-digit number, and make a chain out of the successive results until you get a repeated number. You have found a loop.

For example:

$\boxed{17} \rightarrow 70 - 1 \rightarrow \boxed{69} \rightarrow 90 - 6 \rightarrow \boxed{84} \rightarrow 40 - 8 \rightarrow \boxed{32} \rightarrow 20 - 3 \rightarrow \boxed{17}$

We start and finish with 17. So, we have the loop of 17.

Warning: If you ever have a result which is *not* a two-digit number, then you cannot have a loop – so you stop.

2 Find at least six of these loops.

Describe what you have noticed about each loop.

3 Do you think this will happen with every two-digit number?

Explain your answer.

4 Describe what happens if you change the function to $\boxed{10x + y \rightarrow 9y - x}$.

5 Try other changes. Describe what you notice.

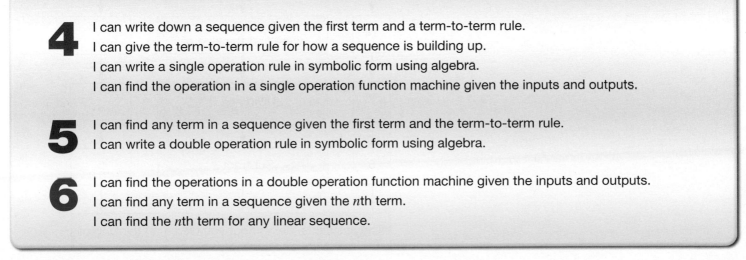

LEVEL BOOSTER

4
I can write down a sequence given the first term and a term-to-term rule.
I can give the term-to-term rule for how a sequence is building up.
I can write a single operation rule in symbolic form using algebra.
I can find the operation in a single operation function machine given the inputs and outputs.

5
I can find any term in a sequence given the first term and the term-to-term rule.
I can write a double operation rule in symbolic form using algebra.

6
I can find the operations in a double operation function machine given the inputs and outputs.
I can find any term in a sequence given the nth term.
I can find the nth term for any linear sequence.

1 *2006 Paper 1*

A ruler costs k pence.
A pen costs m pence.

Match each statement with the correct expression for the amount in pence.

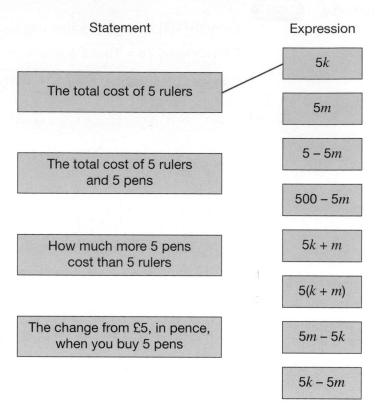

Statement

- The total cost of 5 rulers
- The total cost of 5 rulers and 5 pens
- How much more 5 pens cost than 5 rulers
- The change from £5, in pence, when you buy 5 pens

Expression

- $5k$
- $5m$
- $5 - 5m$
- $500 - 5m$
- $5k + m$
- $5(k + m)$
- $5m - 5k$
- $5k - 5m$

2 *2002 Paper 1*

You can often use algebra to show why a number puzzle works.

Copy this puzzle and fill in the missing expressions.

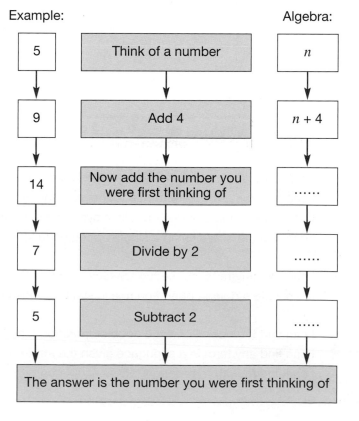

Example:

| 5 |
| 9 |
| 14 |
| 7 |
| 5 |

- Think of a number
- Add 4
- Now add the number you were first thinking of
- Divide by 2
- Subtract 2
- The answer is the number you were first thinking of

Algebra:

- n
- $n + 4$
- ......
- ......
- ......

3   *2004 Paper 1*

    a   A function maps the number *n* to the number $n + 2$.

       Write down the missing values.

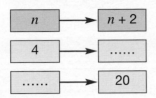

    b   A different function maps the number *n* to the number $2n$.

       Write down the missing values.

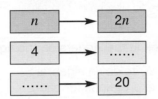

    c   Many different functions can map the number 25 to the number 5.

       Copy and complete the tables by writing two **different** functions.

4   *2006 Paper 2*

    Look at these pairs of number sequences.

    The second sequence is formed from the first sequence by adding a number or multiplying by a number.

    Work out the missing *n*th terms.

    a   5, 9, 13, 17, …   *n*th term is $4n + 1$

       6, 10, 14, 18, …   *n*th term is   …

    b   12, 18, 24, 30, … *n*th term is $6n + 6$

       6, 9, 12, 15, …   *n*th term is   …

    c   2, 7, 12, 17, …   *n*th term is $5n - 3$

       4, 14, 24, 34, …   *n*th term is   …

Valencia Planetarium

Use this key to answer the following questions.

Ladders and grids are made from combinations of:

'L' links   'T' links   'X' links   'R' rods

Each combination can be expressed algebraically.

For example

$4L + 2T + 7R$ $4L + 6T + 2X + 17R$

1 Look at the ladders on the right.

i

ii

iii

a Write down algebraic expressions for each of them.

b Copy and fill in this table.

Ladder	L links	T links	R Rods
1	4	0	4
2	4	2	7
3			
4			
5			

c Write down an algebraic expression for the links and rods in ladder 10.

d Write down an algebraic expression for the links and rods in ladder n.

2 Look at the following rectangles that are 2 squares deep.

i   ii   iii

a Write down algebraic expressions for each of them.

b Copy and complete the following table.

c Write down an algebraic expression for the links and rods in a 2×10 rectangle.

Rectangle	L links	T links	X links	R Rods
2×1	4	2	0	7
2×2	4	4	1	12
2×3				
2×4				
2×5				

d Write down an algebraic expression for the links and rods in a $2 \times n$ rectangle.

3 Look at the following rectangles that are 3 squares deep.

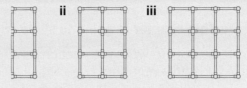

i **ii** **iii**

a Write down algebraic expressions for each of them.

b Copy and complete the following table.

Rectangle	L links	T links	X links	R Rods
3 × 1	4	4	0	10
3 × 2	4	6	2	17
3 × 3				
3 × 4				
3 × 5				

c Write down an algebraic expression for the links and rods in an 3 × 10 rectangle.

d Write down an algebraic expression for the links and rods in a 3 × n rectangle.

4 Using the algebraic expressions for a 2 × n and a 3 × n rectangle in panels 4 and 5, write down an algebraic expression for the number of links and rods in a 4 × n rectangle.

5 Look at the following squares.   **i**   **ii**   **iii**

a Write down algebraic expressions for each of them.

b Copy and complete the following table.

Square	L links	T links	X links	R Rods
1 × 1	4	0	0	4
2 × 2	4	4	1	12
3 × 3				

c Continue the table to find the number of links and rods in a 7 × 7 square.

d Describe how the pattern of T links is building up.

e What type of special numbers are the numbers of X links?

f Show that the number of rods in an $n \times n$ square is given by the nth term $2n(n + 1)$.

g Write down an algebraic expression for the number of links and rods in an 8 × 8 square.

h Write down an algebraic expression for the number of links and rods in an $n \times n$ square.

6 Find the relationship between the number of each type of link and the number of rods.

Hint: Think of the number of connections on each link.

This chapter is going to show you	What you should already know
● How to work with decimals and whole numbers ● How to use estimation to check your answers ● How to solve problems using decimals and whole numbers, with and without a calculator	● How to write and read whole numbers and decimals ● How to write decimal fractions ● Times tables up to 10×10 ● How to use a calculator to do simple calculations

Decimals

Look at this picture. What do the decimal numbers mean? How would you say them?

When you multiply by 100, all the digits are moved two places to the left.

Example 2.1 ▶ Work out 3.5×100.

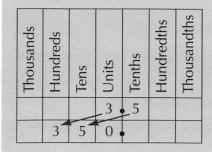

The digits move one place to the left when you multiply by 10, and three places to the left when you multiply by 1000.

When you divide by 1000, all the digits move three places to the right.

Example 2.2 ▶

Work out 23 ÷ 1000.

Thousands	Hundreds	Tens	Units	Tenths	Hundredths	Thousandths
		2	3.			
			0.	0	2	3

In the same way, the digits move one place to the right when you divide by 10, and two places to the right when you divide by 100.

Exercise 2A

① Without using a calculator work out the following.

a	3.4×10	**b**	0.045×10	**c**	0.6×10	**d**	0.89×100
e	0.053×100	**f**	0.03×100	**g**	$0.4 \div 1000$	**h**	$5.8 \div 1000$
i	$3.4 \div 10$	**j**	$0.045 \div 10$	**k**	$0.6 \div 10$	**l**	$0.89 \div 100$

② Fill in the missing operation in each case.

a $0.37 \rightarrow \boxed{} \rightarrow 370$ **b** $567 \rightarrow \boxed{} \rightarrow 0.0567$

c $0.07 \rightarrow \boxed{} \rightarrow 70$ **d** $650 \rightarrow \boxed{} \rightarrow 6.5$

③ Find the missing number in each case.

a $0.03 \times 10 = \boxed{}$ **b** $0.3 \times \boxed{} = 30$ **c** $0.3 \div 10 = \boxed{}$

d $3 \div \boxed{} = 0.03$ **e** $0.3 \times 10 = \boxed{}$ **f** $0.03 \times \boxed{} = 300$

g $0.03 \div 100 = \boxed{}$ **h** $0.3 \div \boxed{} = 0.003$ **i** $\boxed{} \div 100 = 0.03$

④ 10^2 means $10 \times 10 = 100$, 10^3 means $10 \times 10 \times 10 = 1000$.

Copy and complete each of the following.

$10^4 = \ldots \times \ldots \times \ldots \times \ldots = \ldots\ldots$

$10^5 = \qquad\qquad\qquad = \ldots\ldots$

$10^6 = \qquad\qquad\qquad = \ldots\ldots$

⑤ Write down the answers to each of these.

a	3.5×10^2	**b**	0.4×10^3	**c**	0.07×10^2	**d**	2.7×10^5
e	0.6×10	**f**	7.08×10^3	**g**	$3.5 \div 10^2$	**h**	$0.4 \div 10^3$
i	$0.07 \div 10$	**j**	$0.06 \div 10^3$	**k**	$700 \div 10^4$	**l**	$80 \div 10^3$

Extension Work

Design a poster to explain clearly how to multiply and/or divide a number by a power of 10 such as 10^3, 10^5.

Ordering decimals

Name	Leroy	Myrtle	Jack	Baby Jane	Alf	Doris
Age	37.4	21	$32\frac{1}{2}$	9 months	57	68 yrs 3 mths
Height	170 cm	1.54 m	189 cm	0.55 m	102 cm	1.80 m
Weight	75 kg	50.3 kg	68 kg	7.5 kg	85 kg	76 kg 300 g

Look at the people in the picture. How would you put them in order?

When you compare the size of numbers, you have to consider the **place value** of each digit.

It helps if you fill in the numbers in a table like the one shown on the right.

The decimal point separates the whole-number part of the number from the decimal-fraction part.

Thousands	Hundreds	Tens	Units	Tenths	Hundredths	Thousandths	Ten thousandths
			2	3	3	0	
			2	0	3	0	
			2	3	0	4	

Example 2.3 ▷ Put the numbers 2.33, 2.03 and 2.304 in order, from smallest to largest.

The numbers are shown in the table. Zeros have been added to make up the missing decimal places.

Working across the table from the left, you can see that all of the numbers have the same units digit. Two of them have the same tenths digit, and two have the same hundredths digit. But only one has a digit in the thousandths. The order is:

    2.03, 2.304 and 2.33

Example 2.4 ▷ Put the correct sign, > or <, between each of these pairs of numbers.

  a   6.05 and 6.046   **b**   0.06 and 0.065

  a   Both numbers have the same units and tenths digits, but the hundredths digit is bigger in the first number. So the answer is 6.05 > 6.046.

  b   Both numbers have the same units, tenths and hundredths digits, but the second number has the bigger thousandths digit, as the first number has a zero in the thousandths. So the answer is 0.06 < 0.065.

1 a Copy the table on page 18 (but not the numbers). Write the following numbers in the table, placing each digit in the appropriate column.

4.57, 0.0045, 4.057, 4.5, 0.0457, 0.5, 4.05

b Use your answer to part **a** to write the numbers in order from smallest to largest.

2 Write each of these sets of numbers in order from smallest to largest.

a 0.0073, 0.073, 0.008, 0.7098, 0.7

b 1.2033, 1.0334, 1.405, 1.4045, 1.4

c 34, 3.4, 0.34, 0.034, 3.0034

3 Put these amounts of money in order.

a 56p £1.25 £0.60 130p £0.07

b £0.04 £1.04 101p 35p £0.37

4 Put these times in order: 1hour 10 minutes, 25 minutes, 1.25 hours, 0.5 hours

5 One metre is 100 centimetres. Change all the lengths below to metres and then put them in order from smallest to largest.

6.25 m, 269 cm, 32 cm, 2.7 m, 0.34 m

6 One kilogram is 1000 grams. Change all the weights below to kilograms and then put them in order from smallest to largest.

467 g, 1.260 kg, 56 g, 0.5 kg, 0.055 kg

7 Put the correct sign, > or <, between each of these pairs of numbers.

a 0.315 0.325   **b** 0.42 0.402   **c** 6.78 6.709

d 5.25 km 5.225 km   **e** 0.345 kg 0.4 kg   **f** £0.05 7p

8 Write each of the following statements in words.

a 3.1 < 3.14 < 3.142

b £0.07 < 32p < £0.56

Extension Work

Choose a set of five consecutive integers (whole numbers), such as 3, 4, 5, 6, 7.

Use a calculator to work out the **reciprocal** of each of the five numbers. The reciprocal is the number divided into 1. That is:

$1 \div 3, 1 \div 4, 1 \div 5, 1 \div 6, 1 \div 7$

Put the answers in order from smallest to largest.

Repeat with any five two-digit whole numbers, such as 12, 15, 20, 25, 30.

What do you notice?

Directed numbers

Temperature 32 °C
Latitude 17° South
Time 09 30 h GMT

Temperature –13 °C
Latitude 84° North
Time 23 24 h GMT

Look at the two pictures. What are the differences between the temperatures, the latitudes and the times?

All numbers have a sign. Positive numbers have a + sign in front of them although we do not always write it. Negative (or minus) numbers have a – sign in front of them. We *always* write the negative sign.

The positions of positive and negative numbers can be put on a number line, as below.

$$-10 \ -9 \ -8 \ -7 \ -6 \ -5 \ -4 \ -3 \ -2 \ -1 \ 0 \ 1 \ 2 \ 3 \ 4 \ 5 \ 6 \ 7 \ 8 \ 9 \ 10$$

This is very useful, as it helps us to compare positive and negative numbers and also to add and subtract them.

Example 2.5 ▷

Work out the answers to: **a** $3 - 2 - 5$ **b** $-3 - 5 + 4 - 2$

a Starting at zero and 'jumping' along the number line give an answer of –4.

b $-3 - 5 + 4 - 2 = -6$

Example 2.6 ▷

Work out the answers to: **a** $-2 - {+4}$ **b** $-6 - {-3} + {-2}$

a Rewrite as $-2 - 4$ and count along the number line. $-2 - 4 = -6$

b Rewrite as $-6 + 3 - 2$ and count along the number line. $-6 + 3 - 2 = -5$

Example 2.7 ▷

Work out the answers to each of these.

a $-2 \times {+4}$ **b** -6×-3 **c** $-15 \div -5$ **d** $+6 \times -4 \div -2$

a $2 \times 4 = 8$, and $- \ +$ are equivalent to $-$. So, $-2 \times {+4} = -8$.

b $6 \times 3 = 18$, and $- \ -$ are equivalent to $+$. So, $-6 \times -3 = +18$.

c $15 \div 5 = 3$, and $- \ -$ are equivalent to $+$. So $-15 \div -5 = +3$.

d $+6 \times -4 = -24$. So, $-24 \div -2 = +12$.

Exercise 2C

1 Work out the answer to each of these.

a $6 - 9$	**b** $4 - 3$	**c** $2 - 7$	**d** $3 + 9$	**e** $1 - 3$	**f** $4 - 4$
g $-6 + 9$	**h** $-4 - 1$	**i** $-7 - 3$	**j** $-1 + 8$	**k** $-2 - 3$	**l** $-14 + 7$
m $-2 - 3 + 4$		**n** $-1 + 1 - 2$		**o** $-3 + 4 - 7$	**p** $-102 + 103 - 5$

2 Copy each of these calculations and then fill in the missing numbers.

a   3 + +1 = 4   **b**   −2 − +1 = −3   **c**   4 − +2 = 2
   3 + 0 = 3   −2 − 0 = −2   3 − +1 = 2
   3 + −1 = 2   −2 − −1 = −1   2 − 0 = 2
   3 + −2 = ...   −2 − −2 = ...   1 − −1 = ...
   3 + ... = ...   −2 − ... = ...   0 − ... = ...
   3 + ... = ...   −2 − ... = ... − ... = ...

3 Work out the answer to each of these.

a   +3 − +2   **b**   −4 − −3   **c**   +7 − −6   **d**   −7 + −3   **e**   +7 − +3
f   −9 − −5   **g**   −6 + +6   **h**   +6 − −7   **i**   −6 + −6   **j**   −1 + −8
k   +5 − +7   **l**   7 − −5   **m**   −2 − −3 + −4   **n**   − +1 + +1 − +2

4 Find the missing number to make each of these true.

a   +2 + −6 = ☐   **b**   +4 + ☐ = +7   **c**   −4 + ☐ = 0
d   +5 + ☐ = −1   **e**   +3 + +4 = ☐   **f**   ☐ − −5 = +7
g   ☐ − +5 = +2   **h**   +6 + ☐ = 0   **i**   ☐ − −5 = −2
j   +2 + −2 = ☐   **k**   ☐ − +2 = − 4   **l**   −2 + −4 = ☐

5 In a magic square, the numbers in any row, column or diagonal add up to give the same answer. Copy and complete each of these magic squares.

a

−7	0	−8
−2		−3

b

−2		−4
		−3
		−8

c

0		−13	−3
	−5		
−7	−9	−10	
−12			−15

6 Copy and complete each of these patterns.

a   3 × 3 = 9   **b**   3 × −2 = −6   **c**   −2 × +1 = −2
   2 × 3 = 6   2 × −2 = −4   −1 × +1 = ...
   1 × 3 = ...   1 × −2 = ... × +1 = ...
   0 × 3 = ...   0 × −2 = ... × +1 = ...
   ... × 3 = ... × −2 = ... × +1 = ...
   ... × 3 = ... × −2 = ... × +1 = ...

7 Work out the answer to each of these.

a   +2 × −3   **b**   −3 × +4   **c**   −5 × +2   **d**   −6 × −3
e   −3 × +8   **f**   −4 × +5   **g**   −3 × −4   **h**   −6 × −1
i   +7 × −2   **j**   +2 × +8   **k**   +6 × −10   **l**   +8 × +4
m   −15 × −2   **n**   −6 × −3 × −1   **o**   −2 × +4 × −2

8 Work out the answer to each of these.

a $+12 \div -3$	**b** $-24 \div +4$	**c** $-6 \div +2$	**d** $-6 \div -3$
e $-32 \div +8$	**f** $-40 \div +5$	**g** $-32 \div -4$	**h** $-6 \div -1$
i $+7 \div -2$	**j** $+12 \div +6$	**k** $+60 \div -10$	**l** $+8 \div +4$
m $-15 \div -2$	**n** $-6 \times -3 \div -2$	**o** $-2 \times +6 \div -3$	

Extension Work

A maths test consists of 20 questions. Three points are given for a correct answer and two points are deducted if an answer is wrong or not attempted.

Show that it is possible to get a score of zero.

Show clearly that all the possible scores are multiples of 5.

What happens when there are four points for a correct answer and minus two for a wrong answer? Investigate what happens when the points awarded and deducted are changed.

A computer spreadsheet is useful for this activity.

Estimates

UNITED v CITY

CROWD	41 923
SCORE	2 – 1
TIME OF FIRST GOAL	42 min 13 sec
PRICE OF A PIE	95p
CHILDREN	33% off normal ticket prices

Which of the numbers above can be approximated? Which need to be given exactly?

You should have an idea if the answer to a calculation is about the right size or not. There are some ways of checking answers. First, when it is a multiplication, you can check that the final digit is correct. Second, you can round numbers off and do a mental calculation to see if an answer is about the right size. Third, you can check by doing the inverse operation.

Example 2.8 ▶ Explain why these calculations must be wrong.

a $23 \times 45 = 1053$ **b** $19 \times 59 = 121$

a The last digit should be 5, because the product of the last digits is 15. That is, $23 \times 45 = \ldots 5$.

b The answer is roughly $20 \times 60 = 1200$.

Example 2.9 ▷

Estimate the answers to these calculations.

a $\dfrac{21.3 + 48.7}{6.4}$　　b　31.2×48.5　　c　$359 \div 42$　　d　57×0.42

a Round off the numbers on the top to $20 + 50 = 70$. Round off 6.4 to 7. Then $70 \div 7 = 10$.

b Round off to 30×50, which is $3 \times 5 \times 100 = 1500$.

c Round off to $360 \div 40$, which is $36 \div 4 = 9$.

d Round off to 60×0.4, which is $6 \times 4 = 24$.

Example 2.10 ▷

By using the inverse operation, check if each calculation is correct.

a $450 \div 6 = 75$　　b　$310 - 59 = 249$

a By the inverse operation, $450 = 6 \times 75$. This is true and can be checked mentally: $6 \times 70 = 420$, $6 \times 5 = 30$, $420 + 30 = 450$.

b By the inverse operation, $310 = 249 + 59$. This must end in 8 as $9 + 9 = 18$, so it cannot be correct.

Exercise 2D

1 Explain why these calculations must be wrong.

a $24 \times 42 = 1080$　　b　$51 \times 73 = 723$　　c　$\dfrac{34.5 + 63.2}{9.7} = 20.07$

d $360 \div 8 = 35$　　e　$354 - 37 = 323$

2 Amy bought 6 bottles of pop at 46p per bottle. The shopkeeper asked her for £3.16. Without working out the correct answer, explain why this is wrong.

3 A stamp costs 27p. I need eight. Will £2 be enough to pay for them? Explain your answer clearly.

4 Round off each of the following to one decimal place.

a 0.56　　b 0.67　　c 0.89　　d 1.23　　e 3.45
f 1.38　　g 4.72　　h 9.99　　i 0.12　　j 0.07
k 1.46　　l 5.216　　m 8.765　　n 5.032　　o 5.067

5 Work out each of these.

a 60×0.7　　b 50×0.2　　c 90×0.7　　d 30×0.4
e 80×0.4　　f 40×0.8　　g 40×0.2　　h 20×0.9
i 40×0.9　　j 30×0.8　　k 30×0.5　　l 120×0.2

6 Estimate the answer to each of these problems.

a $2768 - 392$　　b 231×18　　c $792 \div 38$　　d $\dfrac{36.7 + 23.2}{14.1}$

e 423×423　　f $157.2 : 38.2$　　g $\dfrac{135.7 - 68.2}{15.8 - 8.9}$　　h $\dfrac{38.9 \times 61.2}{39.6 - 18.4}$

7 Delroy had £10. In his shopping basket he had a magazine costing £2.65, some batteries costing £1.92, and a tape costing £4.99. Without adding up the numbers, how could Delroy be sure he had enough to buy the goods in the basket? Explain a quick way for Delroy to find out if he could afford a 45p bar of chocolate as well.

8 Estimate the answer to each of the following.

a 72 × 0.56	**b** 61 × 0.67	**c** 39 × 0.81	**d** 42 × 0.17
e 57 × 0.33	**f** 68 × 0.68	**g** 38 × 0.19	**h** 23 × 0.91
i 43 × 0.86	**j** 28 × 0.75	**k** 34 × 0.52	**l** 116 × 0.18

9 $62 \div 0.39$ can be approximated as $60 \div 0.4 = 600 \div 4 = 150$. Estimate the answer to each of the following divisions.

a 62 ÷ 0.56	**b** 139 ÷ 0.67	**c** 39 ÷ 0.81	**d** 42 ÷ 0.17
e 57 ÷ 0.33	**f** 68 ÷ 0.68	**g** 38 ÷ 0.19	**h** 178 ÷ 0.91
i 269 ÷ 0.86	**j** 38 ÷ 0.75	**k** 34 ÷ 0.52	**l** 116 ÷ 0.18

Extension Work

The first 15 **square numbers** are 1, 4, 9, 16, 25, 36, 49, 64, 81, 100, 121, 144, 169, 196 and 225. The inverse operation of squaring a number is to find its **square root**. So $\sqrt{121} = 11$. Only the square numbers have integer square roots. Other square roots have to be estimated or found from a calculator.

For example, to find the square root of 30 use a diagram like that on the right, to estimate that $\sqrt{30} \approx 5.48$. (A check shows that $5.48^2 = 30.03$.)

Here is another example. Find $\sqrt{45}$.

The diagram shows that $\sqrt{45} \approx 6.7$. (Check: $6.7^2 = 44.89$)

Use the above method to find $\sqrt{20}$, $\sqrt{55}$, $\sqrt{75}$, $\sqrt{110}$, $\sqrt{140}$, $\sqrt{200}$. Check your answers with a calculator.

Column method for addition, subtraction and multiplication

Look at the picture. What is wrong?

You may have several ways of adding and subtracting numbers, such as estimation or using a number line. Here you will be shown how to set out additions and subtractions using the column method. You may already have learnt about 'lining up the units digit'. This is not strictly correct. What you do is 'line up the decimal points'.

1.2 + 5 + 0.06
= 0.23

```
  1.2
  5
  0.06
  0.23
```

Example 2.11 ▶

Work out, without using a calculator: **a**   3.27 + 14.8   **b**   12.8 – 3.45

a Write the numbers in columns, lining up the decimal points. You should fill the gap with a zero.

$$
\begin{array}{r}
3.27 \\
+\ 14.80 \\
\hline
18.07 \\
\end{array}
$$
$_{1}$

Note the carry digit in the units column, because 2 + 8 = 10.

b Write the numbers in columns and fill the gap with a zero.

$$
\begin{array}{r}
{}^{0\ 1\ 7\ 1}\\
12.80 \\
-\ \ 3.45 \\
\hline
9.35 \\
\end{array}
$$

Note that, because you cannot take 5 from 0, you have to borrow from the next column. This means that 8 becomes 7 and zero becomes 10.

Example 2.12 ▶

Work out 3.14 + 14.5 – 8.72.

This type of problem needs to be done in two stages. First, do the addition and then do the subtraction.

$$
\begin{array}{r}
3.14 \\
+\ 14.50 \\
\hline
17.64 \\
\end{array}
\qquad
\begin{array}{r}
{}^{0\ 16\ 1}\\
17.64 \\
-\ \ 8.72 \\
\hline
8.92 \\
\end{array}
$$

Example 2.13 ▶

Work out: **a**   3.7 × 9   **b**   6.24 × 8

Do these as 'short' multiplications and keep the decimal points lined up.

a
$$
\begin{array}{r}
3.7 \\
\times\ \ \ \ 9 \\
\hline
33.3 \\
\end{array}
$$
$_{6}$

b
$$
\begin{array}{r}
6.24 \\
\times\ \ \ \ \ 8 \\
\hline
49.92 \\
\end{array}
$$
$_{1\ 3}$

Exercise 2E

 By means of a drawing, show how you would use a number line to work out the answers to these.

    a   2.4 + 3.7   **b**   8.4 – 5.6

 Repeat the calculations in Question 1 using the column method. Show all your working.

3 Use the column method to work out the following additions.

    a   37.1 + 14.2   **b**   32.6 + 15.73   **c**   6.78 + 4.59   **d**   9.62 + 0.7

    e   4.79 + 1.2   **f**   6.08 + 2.16   **g**   1.2 + 3.41 + 4.56

    h   76.57 + 312.5 + 6.08

4 Use the column method to work out the following subtractions.

a   37.1 – 14.2   b   32.6 – 15.73   c   6.78 – 4.59   d   9.62 – 0.7

e   4.79 – 1.2   f   6.08 – 2.16   g   1.2 + 3.41 – 4.56

h   76.57 + 312.5 – 6.08

5 Work out the cost of a pair of socks at £4.99, a pair of laces at 79p, a tin of shoe polish at £1.23 and two shoe brushes at £1.34 each.

6 Write the change you would get from £10 if you bought goods worth:

a   £4.56   b   £3.99   c   £7.01   d   34p

7 Use the column method to work out each of the following.

a 2.6×7 b 3.1×9 c 4.8×8 d 4.3×7

e 3.14×3 f 7.06×8 g 6.84×7 h 3.79×5

i 9.26×4 j 8.23×9 k 1.47×9 l 3.89×6

m 6.25×8 n 2.49×5 o 3.65×8 p 9.83×6

8 Work out the cost of six CDs that are £2.95 each.

9 A bar of soap costs £1.37. Work out the cost of seven bars.

10 A bottle of grape juice costs £2.62. Work out the cost of nine bottles.

Extension   **Work**

$6 \times 8 = 48$ $6 \times 0.8 = 4.8$ $0.6 \times 0.8 = 0.48$

When these calculations are set out in columns, they look like this:

```
      8          0.8          0.8
    × 6        × 6.0        × 0.6
    ----       -----        -----
     48          4.8         0.48
```

The column method does not work when we multiply decimals.

Use a calculator to find out the rules for where the decimal point goes in multiplication problems such as:

3×0.2 5×0.7 0.3×0.9 0.2×0.6 0.03×0.5

Solving problems

A bus starts at Barnsley and makes four stops before reaching Penistone. At Barnsley 23 people get on. At Dodworth 12 people get off and 14 people get on. At Silkstone 15 people get off and 4 people get on. At Hoylandswaine 5 people get off and 6 people get on. At Cubley 9 people get off and 8 get on. At Penistone the rest of the passengers get off. How many people are on the bus?

When you solve problems, you need to develop a strategy: that is, a way to go about the problem. You also have to decide which mathematical operation you need to solve it. For example, is it addition, subtraction, multiplication or division or a combination of these? Something else you must do is to read the question fully before starting. The answer to the problem above is one! The driver.

Read the questions below carefully.

Exercise 2F

FM **1** It cost six people £15 to go to the cinema. How much would it cost eight people?

FM **2** Ten pencils cost £4.50. How much would seven pencils cost?

3 30 can be worked out as 33 – 3. Can you find two other ways of working out 30 using three equal digits?

4 Arrange the numbers 1, 2, 3 and 4 in each of these to make the problem correct.

   a $\square + \square = \square + \square$ **b** $\square \times \square = \square\,\square$ **c** $\square\,\square \div \square = \square$

5 A water tank holds 500 litres. How much has been used if there is 143.7 litres left in the tank?

6 Strips of paper are 40 cm long. They are stuck together with a 10 cm overlap.

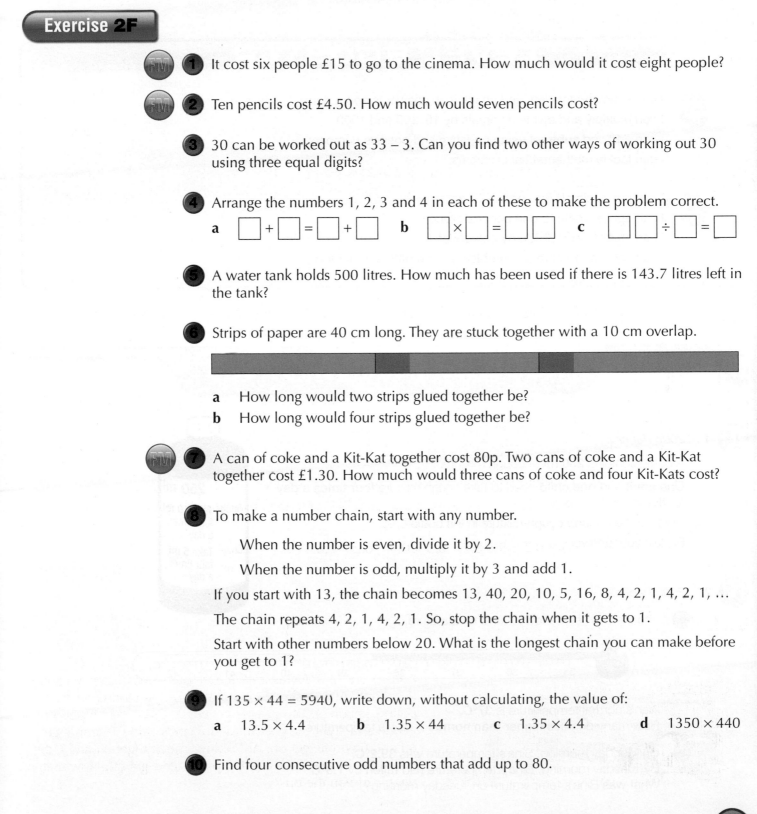

   a   How long would two strips glued together be?
   b   How long would four strips glued together be?

FM **7** A can of coke and a Kit-Kat together cost 80p. Two cans of coke and a Kit-Kat together cost £1.30. How much would three cans of coke and four Kit-Kats cost?

8 To make a number chain, start with any number.

   When the number is even, divide it by 2.

   When the number is odd, multiply it by 3 and add 1.

If you start with 13, the chain becomes 13, 40, 20, 10, 5, 16, 8, 4, 2, 1, 4, 2, 1, …

The chain repeats 4, 2, 1, 4, 2, 1. So, stop the chain when it gets to 1.

Start with other numbers below 20. What is the longest chain you can make before you get to 1?

9 If 135 × 44 = 5940, write down, without calculating, the value of:

   a   13.5 × 4.4   **b**   1.35 × 44   **c**   1.35 × 4.4   **d**   1350 × 440

10 Find four consecutive odd numbers that add up to 80.

Extension Work

Using the numbers 1, 2, 3 and 4 and any mathematical signs, make all of the numbers from 1 to 10.

For example: $2 \times 3 - 4 - 1 = 1$, $12 - 3 - 4 = 5$

Once you have found all the numbers up to 10, can you find totals above 10?

LEVEL BOOSTER

5
I can estimate answers and check if an answer is about right.
I can multiply and divide decimals by 10, 100 and 1000.
I can add and subtract using negative and positive numbers.
I can tackle mathematical problems.

6
I can put decimals into order of size.
I can approximate to one decimal place.
I can multiply and divide by powers of 10.
I can solve more complex problems using different methods.

National Test questions

1 *2006 Paper 2*

A bottle contains **250 ml** of cough mixture.

One adult and **one child** need to take cough mixture **four times a day** for **five** days.

Will there be enough cough mixture in the bottle?

Explain your answer.

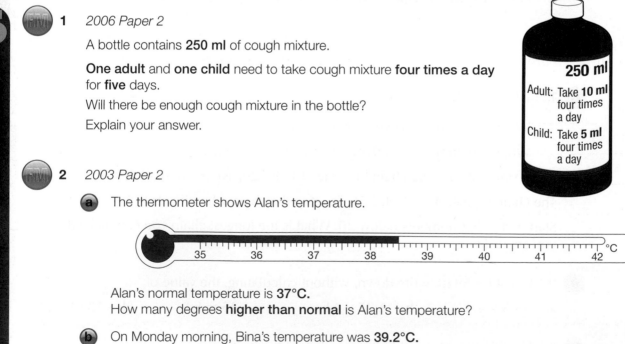

2 *2003 Paper 2*

a The thermometer shows Alan's temperature.

Alan's normal temperature is **37°C**.
How many degrees **higher than normal** is Alan's temperature?

b On Monday morning, Bina's temperature was **39.2°C**.
By Tuesday morning, Bina's temperature had **fallen** by **1.3°C**.
What was Bina's temperature on Tuesday morning?

3   *2005 Paper 1*

a   Look at this information.

> Two numbers **multiply** to make zero.

One of the statements below is true.

Write it down.

Both numbers must be zero.

At least one number must be zero.

Exactly one number must be zero.

Neither number can be zero.

b   Now look at this information.

> Two numbers **add** to make zero.

If **one** number is **zero**, what is the other number?

If **neither** number is **zero**, give an example of what the numbers could be.

c   You can measure temperature in °C or in °F.
The diagram shows how to convert °F to °C.

The highest temperature ever recorded in a human was **115.7°F**.

What is this temperature in **°C**?

Show your working.

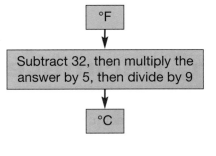

4   *2000 Paper 1*

a   Write the best estimate of the answer to 72.34 ÷ 8.91:   6   7   8   9   10   11

b   Write the best estimate of the answer to 32.7 × 0.48:   1.2   1.6   12   16   120   160

5   *2001 Paper 2*

A drink from a machine costs 55p. The table shows the coins that were put in the machine one day.

Coins	Number of coins
50p	31
20p	22
10p	41
5p	59

How many cans of drink were sold that day?

Exercise 3A

1 Each square on the grid represents one square centimetre. Find the perimeter and area of each shape.

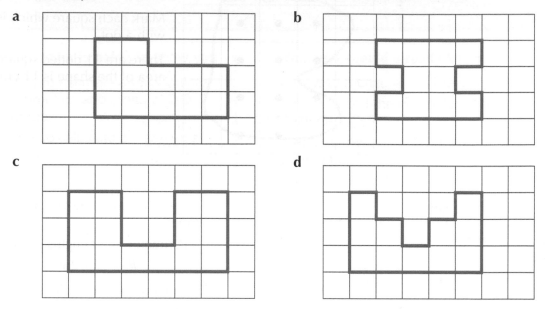

a
b

c
d

2 The following lines are drawn using a scale of 1 cm represents 10 m. Write down the length that each line represents.

a
b
c
d
e

3 Estimate the area of each of these shapes. Each square on the grid represents one square centimetre.

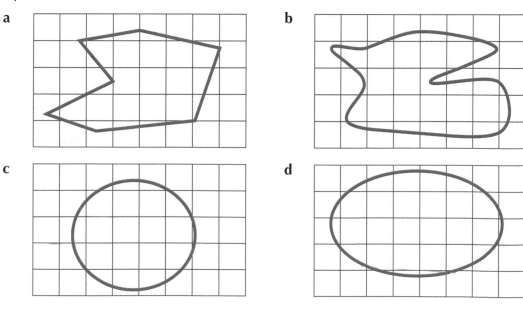

a
b

c
d

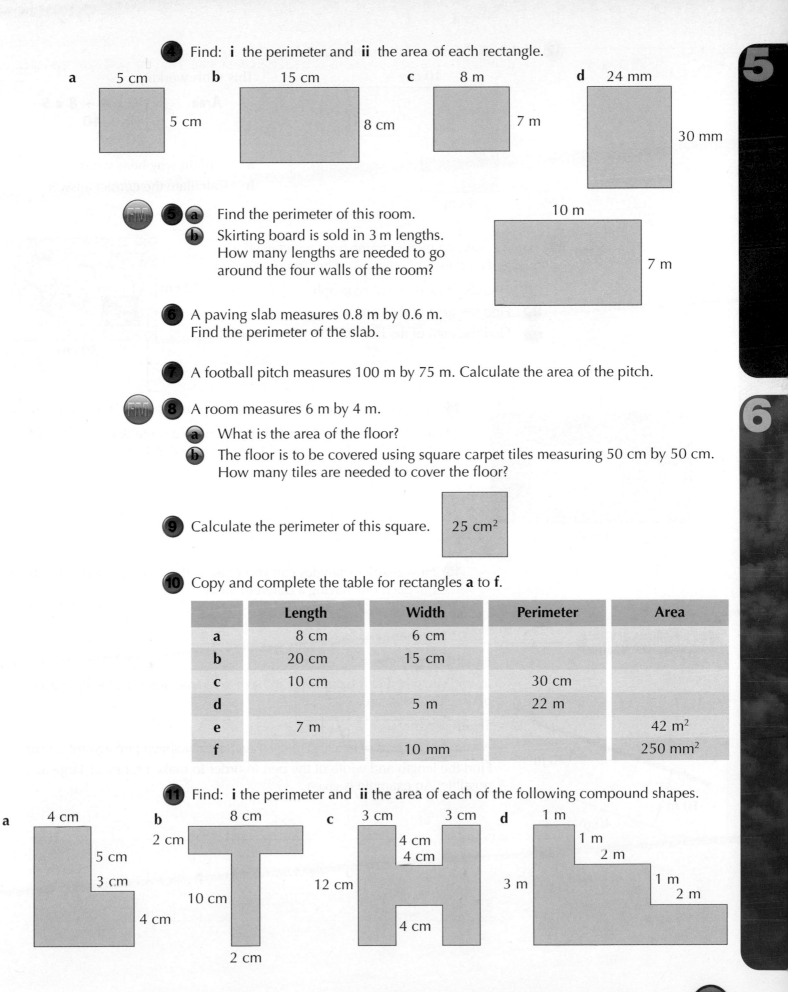

4 Find: **i** the perimeter and **ii** the area of each rectangle.

a 5 cm / 5 cm

b 15 cm / 8 cm

c 8 m / 7 m

d 24 mm / 30 mm

5 **a** Find the perimeter of this room.

b Skirting board is sold in 3 m lengths. How many lengths are needed to go around the four walls of the room?

10 m / 7 m

6 A paving slab measures 0.8 m by 0.6 m. Find the perimeter of the slab.

7 A football pitch measures 100 m by 75 m. Calculate the area of the pitch.

8 A room measures 6 m by 4 m.

a What is the area of the floor?

b The floor is to be covered using square carpet tiles measuring 50 cm by 50 cm. How many tiles are needed to cover the floor?

9 Calculate the perimeter of this square.

25 cm²

10 Copy and complete the table for rectangles **a** to **f**.

	Length	Width	Perimeter	Area
a	8 cm	6 cm		
b	20 cm	15 cm		
c	10 cm		30 cm	
d		5 m	22 m	
e	7 m			42 m²
f		10 mm		250 mm²

11 Find: **i** the perimeter and **ii** the area of each of the following compound shapes.

a 4 cm / 5 cm / 3 cm / 4 cm

b 8 cm / 2 cm / 10 cm / 2 cm

c 3 cm / 3 cm / 4 cm / 4 cm / 12 cm / 4 cm

d 1 m / 1 m / 2 m / 3 m / 1 m / 2 m

12 Phil finds the area of this compound shape.

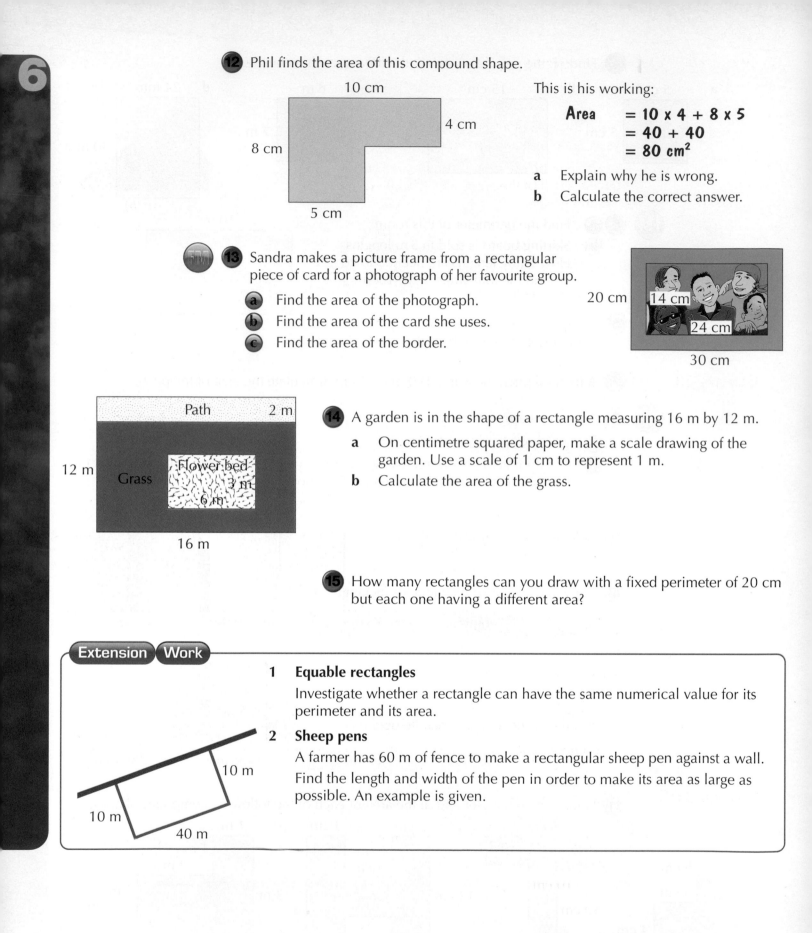

10 cm

4 cm

8 cm

5 cm

This is his working:

Area = 10 x 4 + 8 x 5
= 40 + 40
= **80 cm²**

a Explain why he is wrong.

b Calculate the correct answer.

FM **13** Sandra makes a picture frame from a rectangular piece of card for a photograph of her favourite group.

a Find the area of the photograph.

b Find the area of the card she uses.

c Find the area of the border.

20 cm   14 cm

24 cm

30 cm

Path   2 m

12 m   Grass   Flower bed
3 m
6 m

16 m

14 A garden is in the shape of a rectangle measuring 16 m by 12 m.

a On centimetre squared paper, make a scale drawing of the garden. Use a scale of 1 cm to represent 1 m.

b Calculate the area of the grass.

15 How many rectangles can you draw with a fixed perimeter of 20 cm but each one having a different area?

Extension **Work**

10 m

10 m

40 m

1 **Equable rectangles**

Investigate whether a rectangle can have the same numerical value for its perimeter and its area.

2 **Sheep pens**

A farmer has 60 m of fence to make a rectangular sheep pen against a wall.

Find the length and width of the pen in order to make its area as large as possible. An example is given.

Areas of some 2-D shapes

Area of a triangle

To find the area of a triangle, you need to know the length of its base and its perpendicular height.

The diagram below shows that the area of the triangle is half of the area of a rectangle with the same base and height.

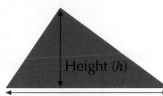

Area 1 = Area 2
Area 3 = Area 4

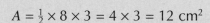

So, the area of a triangle is:

$\frac{1}{2} \times$ Base $\times$ Height

The formula for the triangle is:

$A = \frac{1}{2} \times b \times h = \frac{1}{2}bh$

Example 3.5 ▷

Calculate the area of this triangle.

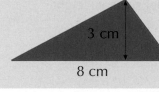

$A = \frac{1}{2} \times 8 \times 3 = 4 \times 3 = 12$ cm^2

Area of a parallelogram

To find the area of a parallelogram, you need to know the length of its base and its perpendicular height.

The diagrams on the right show that the parallelogram has the same area as a rectangle with the same base and height.

So, the area of a parallelogram is:

Base $\times$ Height

The formula for the area of a parallelogram is:

$A = b \times h = bh$

Example 3.6 ▷

Calculate the area of this parallelogram.

$A = 6 \times 10 = 60$ cm^2

Area of a trapezium

To find the area of a trapezium, you need to know the length of its two parallel sides, a and b, and the perpendicular height, h, between the parallel sides.

The diagram below shows how two of the same trapezia fit together to form a parallelogram.

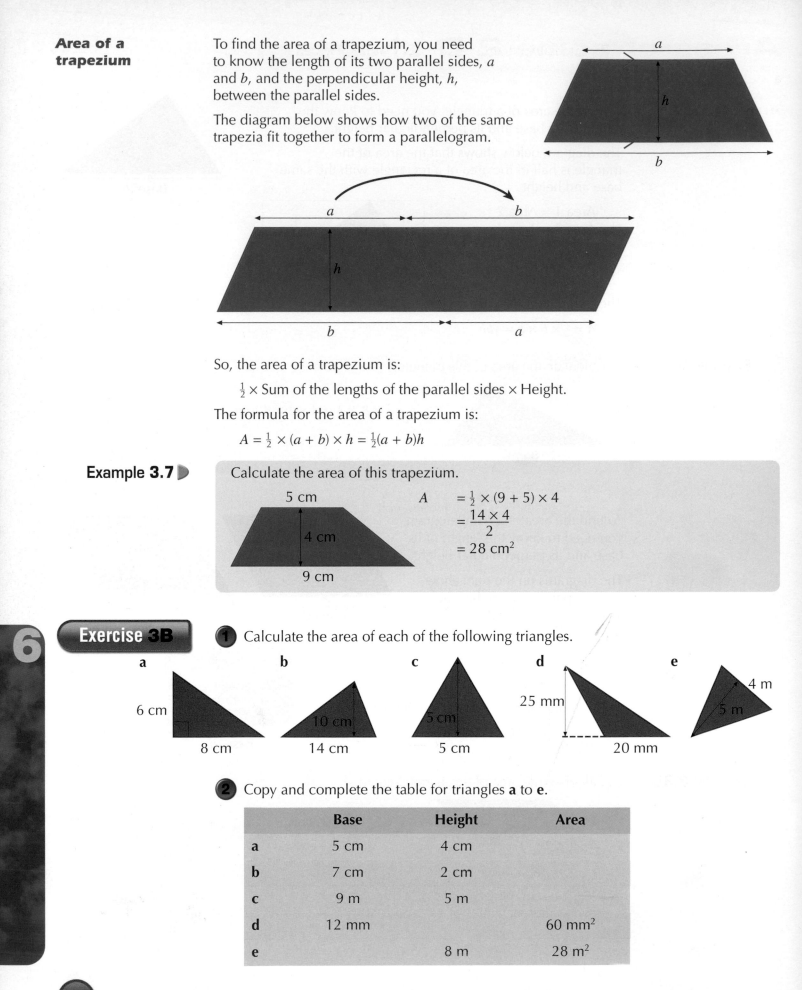

So, the area of a trapezium is:

$\frac{1}{2} \times$ Sum of the lengths of the parallel sides $\times$ Height.

The formula for the area of a trapezium is:

$A = \frac{1}{2} \times (a + b) \times h = \frac{1}{2}(a + b)h$

Example 3.7 ▷

Calculate the area of this trapezium.

5 cm

4 cm

9 cm

$A \quad = \frac{1}{2} \times (9 + 5) \times 4$
$= \dfrac{14 \times 4}{2}$
$= 28 \text{ cm}^2$

Exercise 3B

1. Calculate the area of each of the following triangles.

   a
   6 cm
   8 cm

   b
   10 cm
   14 cm

   c
   5 cm
   5 cm

   d
   25 mm
   20 mm

   e
   4 m
   5 m

2. Copy and complete the table for triangles **a** to **e**.

	Base	Height	Area
a	5 cm	4 cm	
b	7 cm	2 cm	
c	9 m	5 m	
d	12 mm		60 mm²
e		8 m	28 m²

6

3 Calculate the area of each of the following parallelograms.

a 8 cm 12 cm

b 3 m 2.5 m

c 8 cm 15 cm

d 6 mm 18 mm

e 8.4 m 6 m

4 Calculate the area of each of the following trapezia.

a 2 cm 5 cm 12 cm

b 4 cm 8 cm 10 cm

c 5 m 2 m 3 m

d 9 m 5 m 5 m

e 7 mm 16 mm 13 mm

5 The diagram shows the end wall of a garden shed.

   a Find the area of the door.
   b Find the area of the brick wall.

3.5 m

2.5 m

2 m

0.5 m   1 m   0.5 m

6 Find the area of this mathematical stencil with the shapes cut out.

3 cm   6 cm

3 cm   3 cm   3 cm

4 cm

10 cm

6 cm   6 cm

3 cm   3 cm

12 cm

25 cm

7 The area of this trapezium is 8 cm².
   Find different values of *a*, *b* and *h*, with *b* > *a*.

a *h* *b*

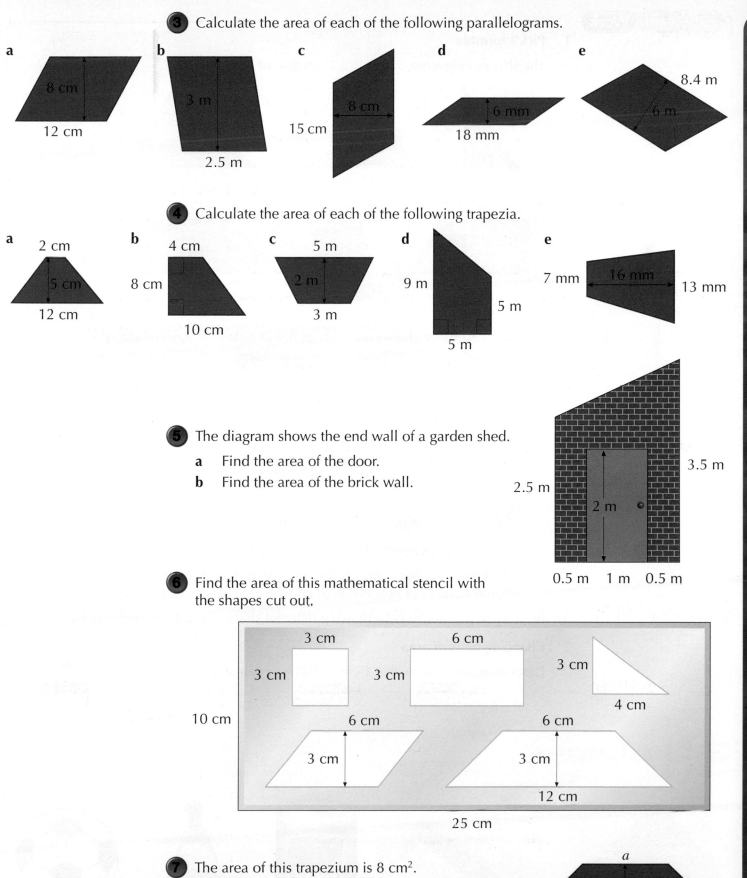

1   Pick's formula

The shapes below are drawn in a 1 cm grid of dots.

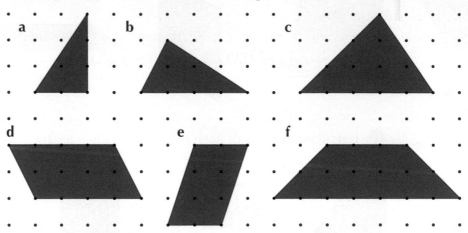

	Number of dots on perimeter of shape	Number of dots inside shape	Area of shape (cm^2)
a			
b			
c			
d			
e			
f			

i   Copy and complete the table for each shape.

ii Find a formula that connects the number of dots on the perimeter (P), the number of dots inside (I) and the area (A) of each shape.

iii Check your formula by drawing different shapes on a 1 cm grid of dots.

2   Changing units of area

Draw diagrams to show that 1 cm^2 = 100 mm^2 and that 1 m^2 = 10 000 cm^2.

3-D shapes

You should be able to recognise and name the following 3-D shapes or solids.

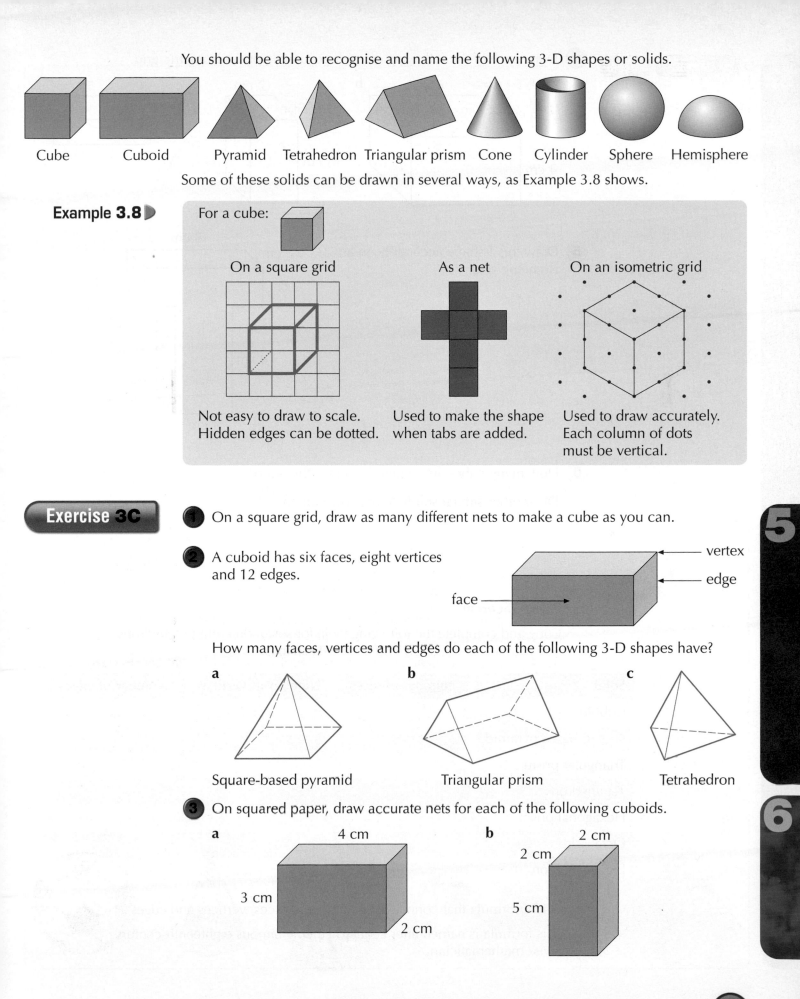

Cube   Cuboid   Pyramid   Tetrahedron   Triangular prism   Cone   Cylinder   Sphere   Hemisphere

Some of these solids can be drawn in several ways, as Example 3.8 shows.

Example 3.8

For a cube:

On a square grid	As a net	On an isometric grid
Not easy to draw to scale. Hidden edges can be dotted.	Used to make the shape when tabs are added.	Used to draw accurately. Each column of dots must be vertical.

Exercise 3C

1. On a square grid, draw as many different nets to make a cube as you can.

2. A cuboid has six faces, eight vertices and 12 edges.

   vertex
   edge
   face

   How many faces, vertices and edges do each of the following 3-D shapes have?

   a   b   c

   Square-based pyramid   Triangular prism   Tetrahedron

3. On squared paper, draw accurate nets for each of the following cuboids.

   a   4 cm   b   2 cm
        3 cm   2 cm
        2 cm   5 cm

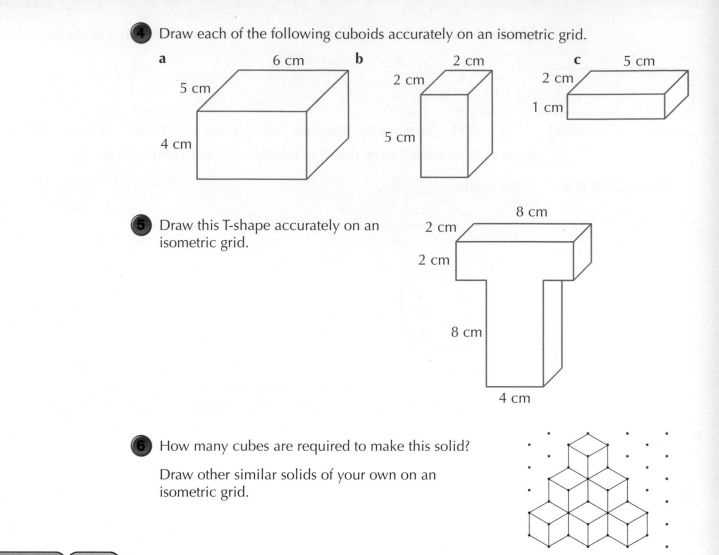

4 Draw each of the following cuboids accurately on an isometric grid.

a 6 cm 5 cm 4 cm

b 2 cm 2 cm 5 cm

c 5 cm 2 cm 1 cm

5 Draw this T-shape accurately on an isometric grid.

2 cm 8 cm 2 cm 8 cm 4 cm

6 How many cubes are required to make this solid?

Draw other similar solids of your own on an isometric grid.

Extension **Work**

1 **Euler's theorem**

Copy and complete the following table for seven different polyhedrons. Ask your teacher to show you these 3-D shapes.

Solid	Number of faces	Number of vertices	Number of edges
Cuboid			
Square-based pyramid			
Triangular prism			
Tetrahedron			
Hexagonal prism			
Octahedron			
Dodecahedron			

Find a formula that connects the number of faces, vertices and edges.

This formula is named after Léonard Euler, a famous eighteenth-century Swiss mathematician.

2 Pentominoes

A pentomino is a 2-D shape made from five squares that touch side to side. Here are two examples.

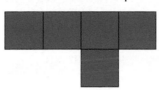 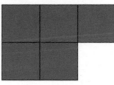

a Draw on squared paper as many different pentominoes as you can.

b How many of these pentominoes are nets that make an open cube?

3 Four cubes

On an isometric grid, draw all the possible different solids that can be made from four cubes. Here is an example.

Surface area and volume of cuboids

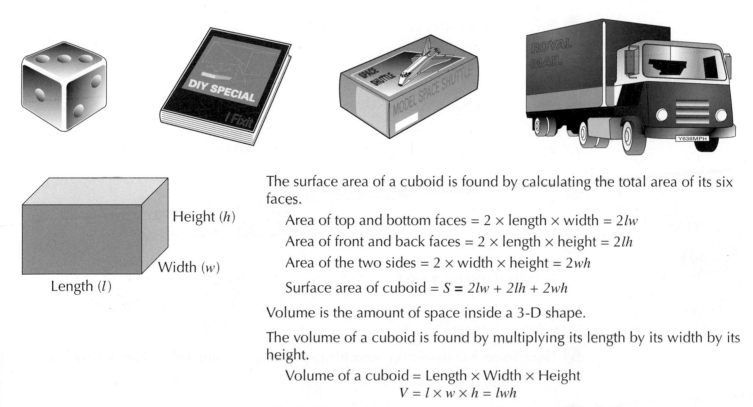

The surface area of a cuboid is found by calculating the total area of its six faces.

Area of top and bottom faces = 2 × length × width = $2lw$

Area of front and back faces = 2 × length × height = $2lh$

Area of the two sides = 2 × width × height = $2wh$

Surface area of cuboid = $S = 2lw + 2lh + 2wh$

Volume is the amount of space inside a 3-D shape.

The volume of a cuboid is found by multiplying its length by its width by its height.

Volume of a cuboid = Length × Width × Height

$$V = l \times w \times h = lwh$$

The metric units of volume in common use are:
cubic millimetre (mm^3)
cubic centimetre (cm^3)
cubic metre (m^3)

Example 3.9 ▶ Find the surface area and volume of this cuboid.

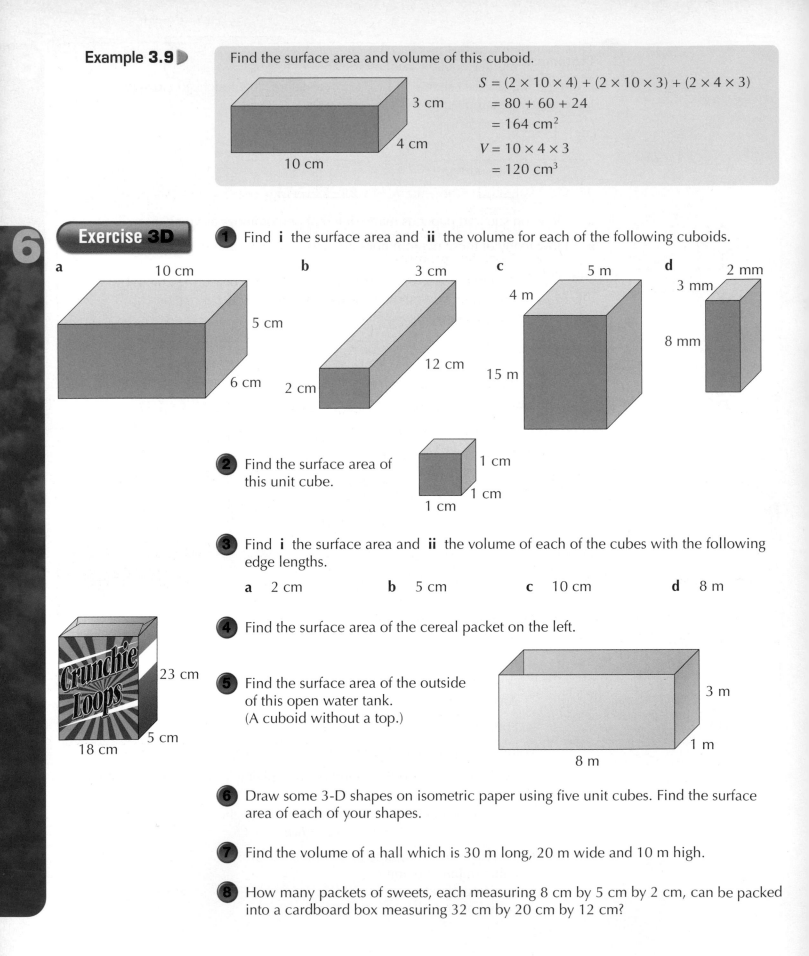

$S = (2 \times 10 \times 4) + (2 \times 10 \times 3) + (2 \times 4 \times 3)$

$= 80 + 60 + 24$

$= 164 \text{ cm}^2$

$V = 10 \times 4 \times 3$

$= 120 \text{ cm}^3$

3 cm

4 cm

10 cm

Exercise 3D

1 Find **i** the surface area and **ii** the volume for each of the following cuboids.

a
10 cm
5 cm
6 cm

b
3 cm
12 cm
2 cm

c
5 m
4 m
15 m

d
2 mm
3 mm
8 mm

2 Find the surface area of this unit cube.

1 cm
1 cm
1 cm

3 Find **i** the surface area and **ii** the volume of each of the cubes with the following edge lengths.

    a   2 cm   **b**   5 cm   **c**   10 cm   **d**   8 m

4 Find the surface area of the cereal packet on the left.

Crunchie Loops
23 cm
5 cm
18 cm

5 Find the surface area of the outside of this open water tank. (A cuboid without a top.)

3 m
1 m
8 m

6 Draw some 3-D shapes on isometric paper using five unit cubes. Find the surface area of each of your shapes.

7 Find the volume of a hall which is 30 m long, 20 m wide and 10 m high.

8 How many packets of sweets, each measuring 8 cm by 5 cm by 2 cm, can be packed into a cardboard box measuring 32 cm by 20 cm by 12 cm?

9 Find the volume of this block of wood, giving your answer in cubic centimetres.

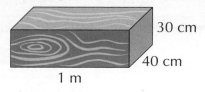

30 cm

40 cm

1 m

Extension **Work**

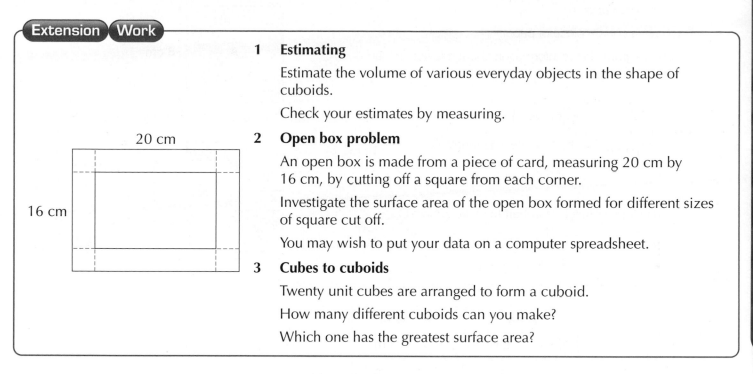

20 cm

16 cm

1 Estimating

Estimate the volume of various everyday objects in the shape of cuboids.

Check your estimates by measuring.

2 Open box problem

An open box is made from a piece of card, measuring 20 cm by 16 cm, by cutting off a square from each corner.

Investigate the surface area of the open box formed for different sizes of square cut off.

You may wish to put your data on a computer spreadsheet.

3 Cubes to cuboids

Twenty unit cubes are arranged to form a cuboid.

How many different cuboids can you make?

Which one has the greatest surface area?

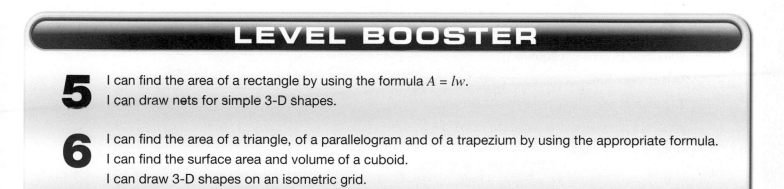

LEVEL BOOSTER

5 I can find the area of a rectangle by using the formula $A = lw$.
I can draw nets for simple 3-D shapes.

6 I can find the area of a triangle, of a parallelogram and of a trapezium by using the appropriate formula.
I can find the surface area and volume of a cuboid.
I can draw 3-D shapes on an isometric grid.

5

1 *2006 4–6 Paper 1*

I have a square piece of paper.

The diagram shows information about this square, labelled A.

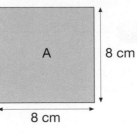

8 cm

8 cm

I fold square A **in half** to make rectangle B.

Then I fold rectangle B **in half** to make square C.

C

Complete the table below to show the area and perimeter of each shape.

	Area	Perimeter
Square A	cm²	cm
Rectangle B	cm²	cm
Square C	cm²	cm

6

2 *2005 Paper 1*

The diagram shows a **square**.

Two straight lines cut the square into four rectangles.

The area of one of the rectangles is shown.

Work out the area of the rectangle marked A.

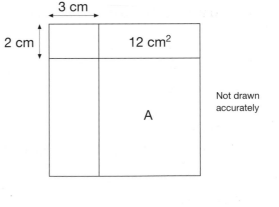

3 cm

2 cm

12 cm²

A

Not drawn accurately

3 *2007 Paper 2*

The diagram shows a shaded parallelogram drawn inside a rectangle.

What is the **area** of the shaded parallelogram?

You **must** give the correct unit with your answer.

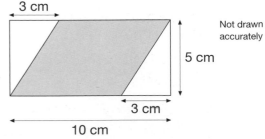

3 cm

Not drawn accurately

5 cm

3 cm

10 cm

4 *2005 Paper 1*

I join six cubes face to face to make each 3-D shape below.

Then I join the 3-D shapes to make a **cuboid**.

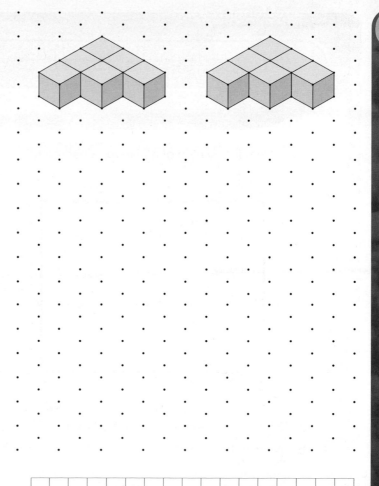

Draw this cuboid on isometric paper or a copy of the grid on the right.

5 *2003 Paper 2*

The squared paper shows the nets of cuboid A and cuboid B.

a Do the cuboids have the same surface area?

Show calculations to explain how you know.

b Do the cuboids have the **same volume**?

Show calculations to explain how you know.

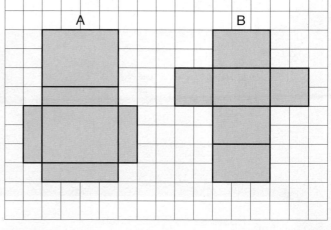

6 *2002 Paper 2*

The drawing shows 2 cuboids that have the **same volume**.

a What is the volume of cuboid A?

Remember to state your units.

b Work out the value of the length marked x.

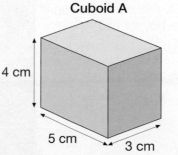

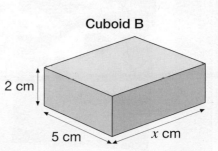

Design a bedroom

1 Here is a sketch of a plan for a bedroom.

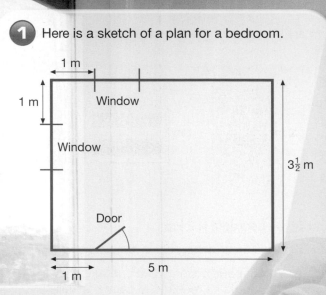

a What is the perimeter of the bedroom?

b What is the area of the bedroom?

c How much does it cost to carpet the bedroom, if 1 m² of carpet costs £32.50?

2 Posters cost £6.99 each.

a How many posters can you buy for £50?

b How much is left over?

Use catalogues or the Internet to find how much it would cost to buy all the furniture for the bedroom.

3 Here are sketches of the door and one of the windows.

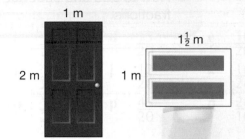

The height of the bedroom is $2\frac{1}{2}$ m.

a What is the total area of the walls in the bedroom?

b If a one-litre tin of paint covers 12 m², what is the minimum number of tins required to paint the walls?

Furniture challenge

4 Copy the plan of the bedroom onto centimetre-squared paper. Use a scale of 1 cm to $\frac{1}{2}$ m.
Decide where you would put the following bedroom furniture. Use cut-outs to help.

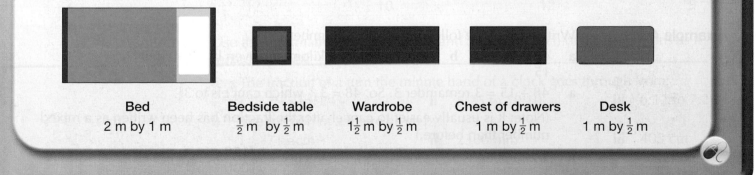

Bed	Bedside table	Wardrobe	Chest of drawers	Desk
2 m by 1 m	$\frac{1}{2}$ m by $\frac{1}{2}$ m	$1\frac{1}{2}$ m by $\frac{1}{2}$ m	1 m by $\frac{1}{2}$ m	1 m by $\frac{1}{2}$ m

This chapter is going to show you

- How to calculate the mode, the median, the mean and the range for a set of data
- How to interpret statistical diagrams and charts
- How to calculate probabilities using equally likely outcomes
- How to collect data from experiments and calculate probabilities

What you should already know

- How to interpret data from tables, graphs and charts
- How to draw line graphs, frequency tables and bar charts

Mode, median and range

Statistics is concerned with the collection and organisation of data, the representation of data on diagrams and the interpretation of data.

When interpreting data we often need to find an **average**. For example: the average rainfall in Britain, the average score of a batsman, the average weekly wage, the average mark in an examination.

An average is a useful statistic because it represents a whole set of values by just a single or typical value. This section explains how to find two types of average: the **mode** and the **median**. It also explains how to find the **range** of a set of values.

The **mode** is the value that occurs most often in a set of data. It is the only average that can be used for non-numerical data. Sometimes there may be no mode because either all the values are different, or no single value occurs more often than other values. For grouped data, a mode cannot be found, so, instead, we find the **modal class**.

The **median** is the middle value for a set of values when they are put in numerical order. It is often used when one value in the set of data is much larger or much smaller than the rest. This value is called a **rogue value**.

The **range** of a set of values is the largest value minus the smallest value. A small range means that the values in the set of data are similar in size, whereas a large range means that the values differ considerably and therefore are more spread out.

Example 5.1 ▷

Here are the ages of 11 players in a football squad. Find the mode, median and range.

23, 19, 24, 26, 28, 27, 24, 23, 20, 23, 26

First, put the ages in order: 19, 20, 23, 23, 23, 24, 24, 26, 26, 27, 28

The mode is the number which occurs most often. So, the mode is 23.

The median is the number in the middle of the set. So, the median is 24.

The range is the largest number minus the smallest number: 28 – 19 = 9. The range is 9.

Example 5.2 ▶ Below are the marks of ten pupils in a mental arithmetic test. Find the mode, median and range.

> 19, 18, 16, 15, 13, 14, 20, 19, 18, 15

First, put the marks in order: 13, 14, 15, 15, 16, 18, 18, 19, 19, 20

There is no mode because no number occurs more often than the others.

There are two numbers in the middle of the set: 16 and 18. The median is the number in the middle of these two numbers. So, the median is 17.

The range is the largest number minus the smallest number: 20 – 13 = 7. The range is 7.

Exercise 5A

1 Find the median and the range of the following sets of data.

   a 7, 6, 2, 3, 1, 9, 5, 4, 8

   b 36, 34, 45, 28, 37, 40, 24, 27, 33, 31, 41

   c 14, 12, 18, 6, 10, 20, 16, 8, 5

   d 99, 101, 107, 103, 109, 102, 105, 110, 100, 98, 99

   e 23, 37, 18, 23, 28, 19, 21, 25, 36

   f 3, 1, 2, 3, 1, 0, 4, 2, 4, 2, 2, 6, 5, 4, 5

   g 2.1, 3.4, 2.7, 1.8, 2.2, 2.6, 2.9, 1.7, 2.3

   h 2, 1, 3, 0, –2, 3, –1, 1, 0, –2, 1

2 Find the mode, median and range of each set of data.

   a £2.50   £1.80   £3.65   £3.80   £4.20   £3.25   £1.80

   b 23 kg, 18 kg, 22 kg, 31 kg, 29 kg, 32 kg

   c 132 cm, 145 cm, 151cm, 132 cm, 140 cm, 142 cm

   d 32°, 36°, 32°, 30°, 31°, 31°, 34°, 33°, 32°, 35°

3 A group of nine Year 7 pupils had their lunch in the school <u>cafeteria</u>.

Given below is the amount that each of them spent.

   £2.30 £2.20 £2.00 £2.50 £2.20 £2.90 £3.60 £2.20 £2.80

   a Find the mode for the data.

   b Find the median for the data.

   c Which is the better average to use?
      Explain your answer.

4 Mr Kent draws a grouped frequency table to show the marks obtained by 32 pupils in his science test.

Mark	Tally	Frequency
21–40	ＪＨＴ	
41–60	ＪＨＴ ＩＩＩＩ	
61–80	ＪＨＴ ＪＨＴ Ｉ	
81–100	ＪＨＴ ＩＩ	

a Copy and complete the frequency column in the table.

b Write down the modal class for Mr Kent's data.

c What is the greatest range of marks possible for the data in the table?

d Explain why it is not possible to find the exact median for the data in the table.

5 **a** Write down a list of seven numbers which has a median of 10 and a mode of 12.

b Write down a list of eight numbers which has a median of 10 and a mode of 12.

c Write down a list of seven numbers which has a median of 10, a mode of 12 and a range of 8.

6 John received an email, but when he printed it out he had lost the final score for each cricketer.

Write down a good estimate of the missing number for each list, giving reasons.

> **Email**
>
> File   Edit   View   Tools   Help
>
> Inbox
>
> **To:** John
> **Subject:** see the following data from our cric
>
> Geff   55, 60, 84, 32, 13, 61, 45, 22, 31,
> mode is 60, median is 55, range is 71
>
> Michael   106, 56, 22, 98, 35, 75, 98, 1
> mode is 98, median is 75, range is 88
>
> Asifusal   67, 83, 29, 9, 110, 120, 121,
> mode is 29, median is 83, range is 130

Extension **Work**

Surveys

Carry out a survey for any of the following. For each one, collect your data on a survey sheet, find the median category and draw diagrams to illustrate your data.

1 The time spent watching TV in a week.

2 The amount spent on lunch in a week.

3 The heights of all the class.

The mean

The **mean** is the most commonly used average. It is also called the **mean average** or simply the **average**. The mean can be used only with numerical data.

The mean of a set of values is the sum of all the values divided by the number of values in the set. That is:

$$\text{Mean} = \frac{\text{Sum of all values}}{\text{Number of values}}$$

The mean is a useful statistic because it takes all values into account, but it can be distorted by rogue values.

Example 5.3 ▷

Find the mean of 2, 7, 9, 10.

$$\text{Mean} = \frac{2 + 7 + 9 + 10}{4} = \frac{28}{4} = 7$$

For more complex data, we can use a calculator. When the answer is not exact, the mean is usually given to one decimal place (1 dp).

Example 5.4 ▷

The ages of seven people are 40, 37, 34, 42, 45, 39, 35. Calculate their mean age.

$$\text{Mean age} = \frac{40 + 37 + 34 + 42 + 45 + 39 + 35}{7} = \frac{272}{7} = 38.9 \text{ (1 dp)}$$

If you don't have a calculator, the mean can sometimes be worked out more quickly by using an **assumed mean**, as the following example shows.

Example 5.5 ▷

Find the mean of 46, 47, 37, 41, 39.

First, choose a value as an initial estimate for the mean. This is the assumed mean and will usually be a central value. It does not have to be a value in the list.

Take the assumed mean for the list to be 40. Then find the difference between each value in the list and the assumed mean. These are 6, 7, −3, 1, −1.

The mean of the differences is:

$$\frac{6 + 7 + -3 + 1 + -1}{5} = \frac{10}{5} = 2$$

(This answer can be negative for some examples.)

The actual mean is:

Assumed mean + Mean of the differences

So, the actual mean for the list of numbers is 40 + 2 = 42.

The mean can also be calculated from a frequency table, as Example 5.6 shows.

Example 5.6 ▶ The frequency table shows the scores obtained when a dice is thrown 20 times. Find the mean score.

Score	1	2	3	4	5	6
Frequency	4	3	4	3	2	4

The table is redrawn in the way shown on the right in order to calculate the sum of the 20 scores.

Score	Frequency	Score × Frequency
1	4	4
2	3	6
3	4	12
4	3	12
5	2	10
6	4	24
Total	**20**	**68**

Mean score = $\frac{68}{20}$ = 3.4

Exercise 5B

1 Find the mean of each of the following sets of data.

   a   8, 7, 6, 10, 4   **b**   23, 32, 40, 37, 29, 25

   c   11, 12, 9, 26, 14, 17, 16   **d**   2.4, 1.6, 3.2, 1.8, 4.2, 2.5, 4.5, 2.2

2 Find the mean of each of the following sets of data, giving your answer to 1 dp.

   a   6, 7, 6, 4, 2, 3   **b**   12, 15, 17, 11, 18, 16, 14

   c   78, 72, 82, 95, 47, 67, 77, 80   **d**   9.1, 7.8, 10.3, 8.5, 11.6, 8.9

3 Use an assumed mean to find the mean of each of the following sets of data.

   a   27, 32, 39, 34, 26, 28

   b   97, 106, 89, 107, 98, 104, 95, 104

   c   237, 256, 242, 251, 238, 259, 245, 261, 255, 236

   d   30.6, 29.8, 31.2, 28.7, 32.8, 29.3, 31.8

4 The heights, in centimetres, of 10 children are:

      132, 147, 143, 136, 135, 146, 153, 132, 137, 149

   a   Find the mean height of the children.

   b   Find the median height of the children.

   c   Find the modal height of the children.

   d   Which average do you think is the best one to use? Explain your answer.

FM **5** The weekly wages of 12 office staff in a small company are:

      £120, £140, £110, £400, £105, £360, £150, £200, £120, £130, £125, £140

   a   Find the mean weekly wage of the staff.

   b   How many staff earn more than the mean wage?

   c   Explain why so few staff earn more than the mean wage.

6 The frequency table shows the shoe sizes of 30 pupils in form 7HW.

Shoe size	3	4	5	6	7	8
Frequency	3	3	8	9	6	1

Calculate the mean shoe size of the form.

7 The bar chart shows the midday temperatures for every day in February for Playa de las Américas in Tenerife.

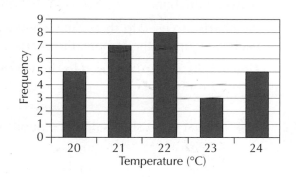

By drawing a suitable frequency table, calculate the mean daily temperature.

8 a 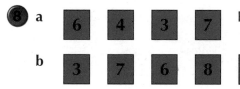 Find the mean of the four cards.

b [3] [7] [6] [8] [?] Find the value of the fifth card, if the mean of the five cards is to be the same as in part **a**.

9 The mean age of three friends, Phil, Martin and Mike, is 42. Steve joins the three and the mean age of the four friends is now 40. How old is Steve?

Extension Work

1 Vital statistics

Working in groups, calculate the mean for the group's age, height and weight.

2 Average score

Throw a dice ten times. Record your results on a survey sheet. What is the mean score?

Repeat the experiment but throw the dice 20 times. What is the mean score now?

Repeat the experiment but throw the dice 50 times. What is the mean score now?

Write down anything you notice as you throw the dice more times.

Statistical diagrams

Once data has been collected from a survey, it can de displayed in various ways to make it easier to understand and interpret.

The most common ways to display data are bar charts, pie charts and line graphs.

Bar charts have several different forms. The questions in Exercise 5C will show you the different types of bar chart that can be used. Notice that data which has single categories gives a bar chart with gaps between the bars. Grouped data gives a bar chart with no gaps between the bars.

Pie charts are used to show data when you do not need to know the number of items in each category of the sample. Pie charts are used to show proportions.

Line graphs are usually used to show trends and patterns in the data.

Exercise 5C

1 The bar chart shows how the pupils in class 7PB travel to school.

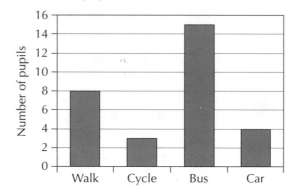

a How many pupils cycle to school?
b What is the mode for the way the pupils travel to school?
c How many pupils are there in class 7PB?

FM **2** The dual bar chart shows the daily average number of hours of sunshine in London and Edinburgh over a year.

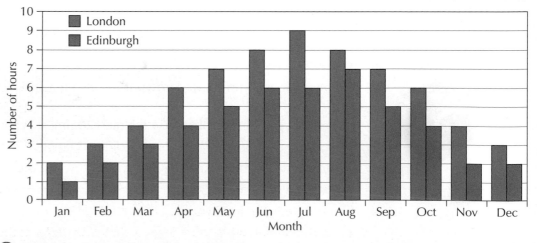

a Which city has the most sunshine?
b Which are the sunniest months?
c How much more sunshine does London usually have than Edinburgh?

3 The percentage compound bar chart shows the favourite colours for a sample of Year 7 pupils.

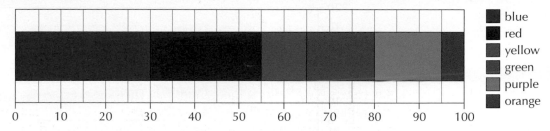

blue
red
yellow
green
purple
orange

a Which is the colour preferred by most pupils?

b What percentage of the pupils preferred yellow?

c Which two colours were equally preferred by the pupils?

d If there were 40 pupils in the sample, how many of them preferred red?

e Explain why the compound bar chart is a useful way to illustrate the data.

4 The bar chart shows the marks obtained in a mathematics test by the pupils in class 7KG.

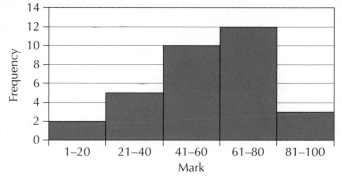

a How many pupils are there in class 7KG?

b What is the modal class for the data?

c How many pupils got a mark over 60?

d Write down the smallest and greatest range of marks possible for the data.

e Ali estimated the mean of the 12 pupils in the 61–80 age group was 70.5. Explain how she might have calculated this estimate.

5 The pie chart shows the TV channel that 60 people in a survey most often watched.

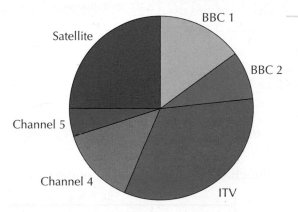

a Which is the most popular channel?

b Which is the least popular channel?

c Which channel is most often watched by 25% of the people in the survey?

d About how many people in the survey most often watched ITV?

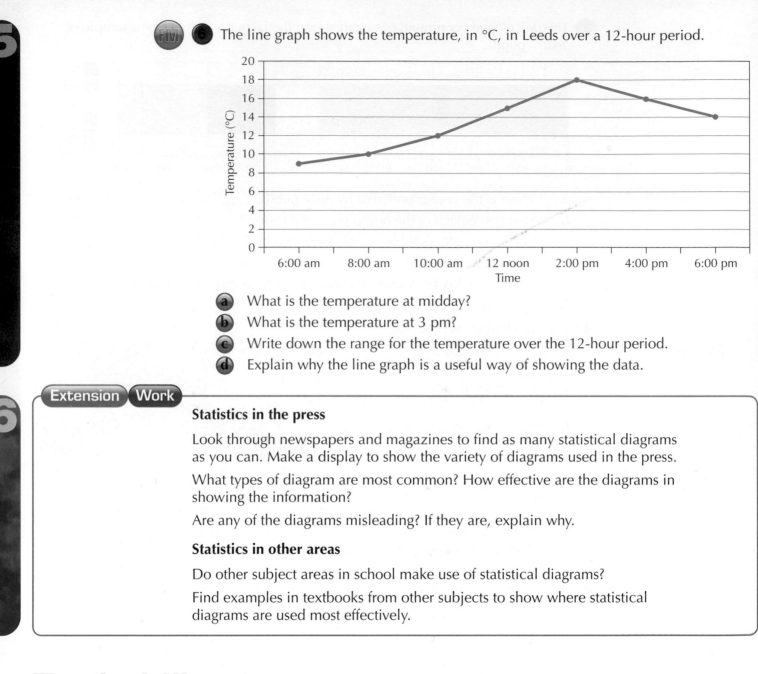

6 The line graph shows the temperature, in °C, in Leeds over a 12-hour period.

a) What is the temperature at midday?

b) What is the temperature at 3 pm?

c) Write down the range for the temperature over the 12-hour period.

d) Explain why the line graph is a useful way of showing the data.

Extension Work

Statistics in the press

Look through newspapers and magazines to find as many statistical diagrams as you can. Make a display to show the variety of diagrams used in the press.

What types of diagram are most common? How effective are the diagrams in showing the information?

Are any of the diagrams misleading? If they are, explain why.

Statistics in other areas

Do other subject areas in school make use of statistical diagrams?

Find examples in textbooks from other subjects to show where statistical diagrams are used most effectively.

Probability

Probability is the way of describing and measuring the chance or likelihood that an event will happen.

The chance of an event happening can be shown on a **probability scale**:

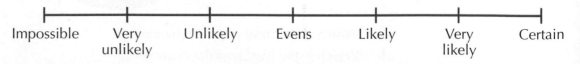

An evens chance is often referred to as 'a 50–50 chance'. Other everyday words used to describe probability are: uncertain, possible, probable, good chance, poor chance.

To measure probability, we use a scale from 0 to 1. So probabilities are written as fractions or decimals, and sometimes as percentages, as in the weather forecasts.

The probability scale is now drawn as:

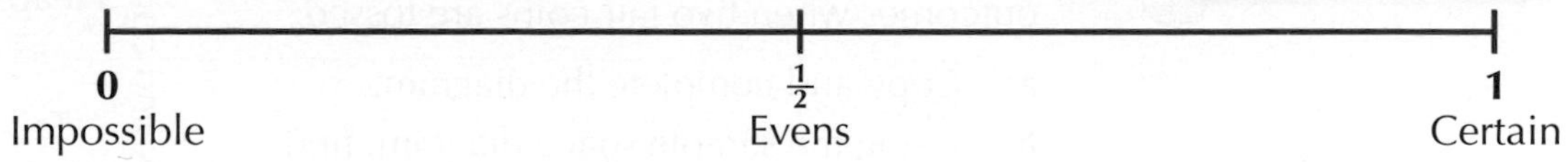

$$\begin{array}{ccc} \mathbf{0} & \frac{1}{2} & \mathbf{1} \\ \text{Impossible} & \text{Evens} & \text{Certain} \end{array}$$

We define the probability of an event happening as:

$$P(\text{event}) = \frac{\text{Number of outcomes in the event}}{\text{Total number of all possible outcomes}}$$

Example 5.7 ▷

When tossing a fair coin, there are two possible outcomes:
Head (H) or Tail (T)

Each outcome is **equally likely** to happen because it is a fair coin. So:

$P(H) = \frac{1}{2}$ and $P(T) = \frac{1}{2}$

This is the **probability fraction** for the event.

(Sometimes, people may say a 1 in 2 chance or a 50–50 chance.)

Example 5.8 ▷

When throwing a fair dice, there are six equally likely outcomes: 1, 2, 3, 4, 5, 6.

So, for example:

$P(6) = \frac{1}{6}$ and $P(1 \text{ or } 2) = \frac{2}{6} = \frac{1}{3}$

Probability fractions are *always* cancelled down.

Example 5.9 ▷

When drawing a card from a normal pack of 52 playing cards, the probability of picking a Spade is:

$P(\text{a Spade}) = \frac{13}{52} = \frac{1}{4}$

So, the probability of *not* picking a Spade is:

$P(\text{not a Spade}) = \frac{39}{52} = \frac{3}{4}$

The answer in Example 5.9 is the same as $1 - \frac{1}{4}$.

So, when the probability of an event occurring is p, the probability of the event not occurring is $1 - p$.

A **sample space diagram** is often used to show the equally likely outcomes for two combined events.

Example 5.10 ▷

The sample space diagram on the right shows all the possible outcomes for the total score when two fair dice are thrown.

The sample space diagram shows that there are 36 equally likely outcomes. So, for example:

a $P(\text{double } 6) = P(\text{score of } 12) = \frac{1}{36}$

b $P(\text{score of } 8) = \frac{5}{36}$

c $P(\text{score greater than } 10) =$
$P(\text{score of } 11 \text{ or } 12) = \frac{3}{36} = \frac{1}{12}$

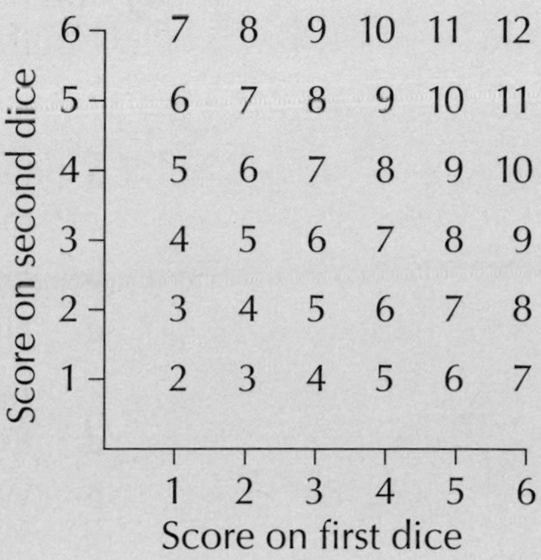

	1	2	3	4	5	6
6	7	8	9	10	11	12
5	6	7	8	9	10	11
4	5	6	7	8	9	10
3	4	5	6	7	8	9
2	3	4	5	6	7	8
1	2	3	4	5	6	7

Score on second dice

Score on first dice

Exercise 5D

1. The sample space diagram shows the outcomes when two fair coins are tossed.

   a Copy and complete the diagram.

   b Using the sample space diagram, find each of the following probabilities.

   i P(2 Heads) **ii** P(2 Tails)

   iii P(1 Head and 1 Tail)

   iv P(not getting 2 Heads)

   Second coin

   Head –

   Tail –   (T, T)

   Tail   Head
   First coin

2. Marion says that the result of a football match can be win, lose or draw. She then says that, since there are three outcomes, …

   Is she correct? Explain your answer.

   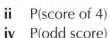

   … the probability that a team wins a match is $\frac{1}{3}$

3. The two different, fair, five-sided spinners shown here are spun together and the product of their scores is recorded.

   a Draw a sample space diagram to show all the possible outcomes.

   b How many equally likely outcomes are there?

   c Find each of the following probabilities.

   i P(score of 18) **ii** P(score of 4)

   iii P(score that is a multiple of 3) **iv** P(odd score)

4. **a** Draw a sample space to show all the possible outcomes for the total of two normal fair dice.

   b Find the probability of rolling a total:

   i less than 6   **ii** equal to 6   **iii** greater than 6

   c **i** Add together the three probabilities in part **b**.

   ii Comment on your result.

   d What is the probability of rolling a total that is NOT a total of 7?

5. You have two dice:

   Dice A showing 0, 1, 1, 2, 2, 3
   Dice B showing 0, 2, 3, 3, 4, 5

   a Draw a sample space to show all the possible outcomes for the PRODUCT of the two dice (product is when numbers are multiplied).

   b Find the probability of rolling a product of 6.

   c Find the probability of rolling:

   i an even product   **ii** an odd product

   d Comment on the sum of the probabilities in part c.

   e What is the probability of rolling a product that is NOT 4?

You will need a set of cards numbered 1 to 10 for this experiment.

Line up the cards, face down and in random order.

1   Turn over the first card.

2   Work out the probability that the second card will be higher than the first card.

3   Work out the probability that the second card will be lower than the first card.

4   Turn over the second card.

5   Work out the probability that the third card will be higher than the second card.

6   Work out the probability that the third card will be lower than the second card.

7   Carry on the process. Write down all your results clearly and explain any patterns that you notice.

Repeat the experiment. Are your results the same?

Experimental probability

The probabilities in the previous section were calculated using equally likely outcomes. A probability worked out this way is known as a **theoretical probability**.

Sometimes, a probability can be found only by carrying out a series of experiments and recording the results in a frequency table. The probability of the event can then be estimated from these results. A probability found in this way is known as an **experimental probability**.

To find an experimental probability, the experiment has to be repeated a number of times. Each separate experiment carried out is known as a **trial**.

$$\text{Experimental probability of an event} = \frac{\text{Number of times the event occurs}}{\text{Total number of trials}}$$

It is important to remember that when an experiment is repeated, the experimental probability will be slightly different each time. The experimental probability of an event is an estimate for the theoretical probability. As the number of trials increases, the value of the experimental probability gets closer to the theoretical probability.

Example 5.11 ▷

A dice is thrown 50 times. The results of the 50 trials are shown in a frequency table.

Score	1	2	3	4	5	6
Frequency	8	9	8	10	7	8

The experimental probability of getting a $3 = \frac{8}{50} = \frac{4}{25}$.

Exercise 5E

1 Working in pairs, toss a coin 50 times and record your results in a frequency table.

a   Use your results to find the experimental probability of getting a Head.

b   What is the theoretical probability of getting a Head?

c   How many Heads would you expect to get after tossing the coin 50 times?

2 Working in pairs, throw a dice 100 times and record your results in a frequency table.

    a   Find the experimental probability of getting 6, writing your answer as:
       i   a fraction   **ii**   a decimal

    b   The theoretical probability of getting a 6 is $\frac{1}{6}$ or 0.17. How close is your experimental probability to the theoretical probability?

    c   Explain how you could improve the accuracy of your experimental probability.

3 Working in pairs, drop a drawing pin 50 times. Record your results in the following frequency table.

	Tally	Frequency
Point up		
Point down		

    a   What is the experimental probability that the drawing pin will land point-up?

    b   Is your answer greater or less than an evens chance?

    c   Explain what would happen if you repeated the experiment.

4 Brian says: 'When I drop a piece of toast, it always lands butter-side down'.

Simulate Brian's statement by dropping a playing card 50 times and recording the number of times the card lands face down.

    a   What is the experimental probability that the card lands face down?

    b   Do you think this is a good way to test Brian's statement? Explain your answer.

5 Working in pairs, toss three coins 50 times. Record, in a frequency table, the number of Heads you get for each trial.

    a   What is the experimental probability of getting each of the following?
       i   three Heads   **ii**   two Heads   **iii**   one Head   **iv**   no Heads

    b   List all the equally likely outcomes for throwing three coins. (Hint: there are eight.) What is the theoretical probability of getting each of the following?
       i   three Heads   **ii**   two Heads   **iii**   one Head   **iv**   no Heads

Extension Work

Biased spinners

Make a six-sided spinner from card and a cocktail stick.

Weight it by sticking a small piece of Plasticine below one of the numbers on the card. This will make the spinner unfair or biased.

Roll the spinner 60 times and record the scores in a frequency table.

Find the experimental probability for each score.

Compare your results with what you would expect from a fair, six-sided spinner.

Repeat the experiment by making a spinner with a different number of sides.

5
I can find the mean and median for a set of data.
I can find the mean from a frequency table.
I can interpret pie charts.
I can calculate probabilities using equally likely outcomes.
I can calculate probability from experimental data.

6
I can calculate probabilities from sample spaces.
I can use the probability of an event to calculate the probability that the event does not happen.

National Test questions

1 *2000 Paper 2*

A newspaper predicts what the ages of secondary school teachers will be in six years' time.

They print this chart.

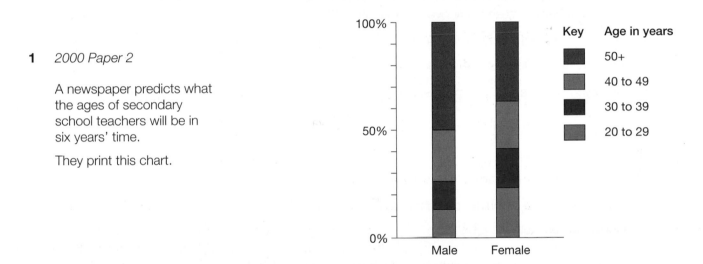

a The chart shows 24% of male teachers will be aged 40 to 49.

About what percentage of female teachers will be aged 40 to 49?

b About what percentage of female teachers will be aged 50+?

c The newspaper predicts there will be about 20 000 male teachers aged 40 to 49.

Estimate the number of male teachers that will be aged 50+.

d Assume the total number of male teachers will be about the same as the total number of female teachers.

Use the chart to decide which statement given below is correct.

Generally, male teachers will tend to be younger than female teachers.

Generally, female teachers will tend to be younger than male teachers.

Explain how you used the chart to decide.

2 *2000 Paper 2*

In each box of cereal there is a free gift of a card.

You cannot tell which card will be in a box. Each card is equally likely.

There are four different cards: A, B, C or D

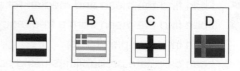

a Zoe needs card A.

Her brother Paul needs cards C and D.

They buy one box of cereal.

What is the probability that the card is one that Zoe needs?

What is the probability that the card is one that Paul needs?

b Then their mother opens the box. She tells them the card is not card A.

Now what is the probability the card is one that Zoe needs?

What is the probability that the card is one that Paul needs?

3 *2000 Paper 2*

a Paula played four games in a competition. In three games, Paula scored 8 points each time. In the other game she scored no points.

What was Paula's mean score over the four games?

b Jessie only played two games. Her mean score was 3 points. Her range was 4 points.

What points did Jessie score in her two games?

c Ali played three games. His mean score was also 3 points. His range was also 4 points.

What points might Ali have scored in his three games? Show your working.

4 *2007 Paper 1*

In a bag there are only red, blue and green counters.

a I am going to take a counter out of the bag at random.

Copy and complete the table below.

Colour of counters	Number of counters	Probability
Red	6	
Blue		$\frac{1}{5}$
Green	6	

b Before I take a counter out of the bag, I put **one extra blue** counter into the bag.

What effect does this have on the probability that I will take a **red** counter?

Write down the correct statement.

The probability has increased.

The probability has decreased.

The probability has stayed the same.

It is impossible to tell.

5 *2006 Paper 1*

Hanif asked ten people:

'What is your favourite sport?'

Here are his results.

football	cricket	football	hockey	swimming
hockey	swimming	football	netball	football

a Is it possible to work out the **mean** of these results?

Explain how you know.

b Is it possible to work out the **mode** of these results?

Explain how you know.

School sports day

Teams

1 Ruskin team has seven members with the following ages:

	Age (years)
Joe	14
Kristen	15
Simon	13
Vikas	15
Helen	14
Sarah	13
Quinn	13

a What is the modal age?

b What is the median age?

c What is the mean age?

100 m sprint

2 The girls' 100 m race was run in the following times:

	Time (seconds)
Kate	22
Kerry	25
Maria	21
Oi Yin	25
Sara	23

a What is the modal time?

b What is the median time?

c What is the mean time?

Long jump

3 Alex had ten practice attempts at the long jump. The bar chart illustrates the range of lengths he jumps.

Range of jumps

He is now prepared for his last long jump.

What is the probability that Alex jumps:

a in the 141–160 cm range?

b longer than 120.5 cm?

c less than 140.5 cm?

Rounders competition

4 In the rounders game between Huntsman and Chantry, the following scorecards were produced as tallies. A tally was put next to a player each time they scored a rounder.

Huntsman		Frequency		Chantry		Frequency
Afzal	HHt	___		Ellen	IIII	___
Claire	II	___		Cynthia	II	___
Gilbert	III	___		Runuka	HHt I	___
John	HHt II	___		Joanne	II	___
Ali	I	___		Michael	I	___
Izolda	I	___		Emily	II	___
Kate	III	___		Julie	HHt II	___
Joy	HHt HHt I	___		Kay	HHt	___
Mari	II	___		Sue	III	___

a What was the modal number of rounders scored by the players?

b What was the mean number of rounders scored for the Huntsman team?

This chapter is going to show you

- How to use letters in place of numbers
- How to use the rules (conventions) of algebra
- How to solve puzzles called equations
- How to solve problems using algebra

What you should already know

- Understand and be able to apply the rules of arithmetic
- The meaning of the words term and expression

Algebraic terms and expressions

In algebra, you will keep meeting three words: **variable**, **term** and **expression**.

Variable This is the letter in a term or an expression whose value can vary. Some of the letters most used for variables are x, y, n and t.

Term This is an algebraic quantity which contains only a letter (or combination of letters) and may contain a number. For example:

$3n$ means 3 multiplied by the variable n

$\frac{n}{2}$ means n divided by 2

n^2 means n multiplied by itself (normally said as 'n squared')

Expression This is a combination of letters (variables) and signs, often with numbers. For example:

$8 - n$ means subtract n from 8

$n - 3$ means subtract 3 from n

$2n + 7$ means n multiplied by 2 with 7 added on

When you give a particular value to the variable in an expression, the expression takes on a particular value.

For example, if the variable n takes the value of 4, then the terms and expressions which include this variable will have particular values, as shown below:

$3n = 12$ $\frac{n}{2} = 2$ $n^2 = 16$ $8 - n = 4$ $n - 3 = 1$ $2n + 7 = 15$

Exercise 6A

1 Write terms, or expressions, to illustrate the following sentences.

a Multiply m by three and add four.

b Multiply t by eight and subtract five.

c Divide y by two and add six.

4

d   Multiply m by itself and subtract three.

e   Divide n by five and subtract one.

f   Add five to m then multiply by two.

g   Subtract four from x then multiply by three.

h   Add two to y then divide by five.

i   Add the square of x to the square of y.

j   Subtract t from seven and multiply by two.

2   Write down the values of each expression for the three values of n.

   a $n^2 - 1$ where   **i** $n = 2$ **ii** $n = 3$ **iii** $n = 4$

   b $5 + n^2$ where   **i** $n = 8$ **ii** $n = 9$ **iii** $n = 10$

   c $n^2 + 9$ where   **i** $n = 5$ **ii** $n = 4$ **iii** $n = 3$

   d $25 + n^2$ where   **i** $n = 4$ **ii** $n = 5$ **iii** $n = 6$

3   Work out the value of the following expressions for the given values of n.

   a $(n + 2)(n - 1)$ where   **i** $n = 3$ **ii** $n = 5$ **iii** $n = 8$

   b $(n - 3)(n + 1)$ where   **i** $n = 5$ **ii** $n = 7$ **iii** $n = 9$

   c $(n - 5)(n - 2)$ where   **i** $n = 6$ **ii** $n = 10$ **iii** $n = 12$

   d $(n + 2)(n + 5)$ where   **i** $n = 3$ **ii** $n = 4$ **iii** $n = 8$

   e $(n + 3)^2$ where   **i** $n = 2$ **ii** $n = 6$ **iii** $n = 7$

4   **a**   Work out the value of the following expressions for the given values of n.

     A $(n + 3)(n - 2)$ where   **i** $n = -3$ **ii** $n = 2$

     B $(n - 4)(n + 5)$ where   **i** $n = 4$ **ii** $n = -5$

     C $(n - 3)(n - 2)$ where   **i** $n = 3$ **ii** $n = 2$

   b   What do you notice about the answer to part **a**?

   c   Write down the two values of n that will make the values of these expressions zero.

     i $(n - 6)(n - 1)$ **ii** $(n + 1)(n + 7)$

     iii $(n - 5)(n + 6)$ **iv** $(n + 2)(n - 8)$

Extension **Work**

1   Work out the value of $a^2 - b^2$ for:

   i $a = 5$ and $b = 3$ **ii** $a = 8$ and $b = 2$ **iii** $a = 7$ and $b = 4$

   iv $a = 10$ and $b = 1$ **v** $a = 9$ and $b = 6$

2   Work out the value of $(a - b)(a + b)$ for:

   i $a = 5$ and $b = 3$ **ii** $a = 8$ and $b = 2$ **iii** $a = 7$ and $b = 4$

   iv $a = 10$ and $b = 1$ **v** $a = 9$ and $b = 6$

3   What do you notice about your answers for questions **1** and **2**?

   $(a - b)(a + b) = a^2 - b^2$ is called an identity because it is true for all values.

4   By trying several different values for a and b, find out if the following are identities.

   a $(a + b)^2 = a^2 + b^2$ **b** $(a - b)^2 = a^2 - 2ab + b^2$

Rules of algebra

The rules (conventions) of algebra are the same rules that are used in arithmetic.
For example:

$3 + 4 = 4 + 3$ $a + b = b + a$
$3 \times 4 = 4 \times 3$ $a \times b = b \times a$ or $ab = ba$

But remember, for example, that:

$7 - 5 \neq 5 - 7$ $a - b \neq b - a$
$6 \div 3 \neq 3 \div 6$ $\dfrac{a}{b} \neq \dfrac{b}{a}$

From one fact, other facts can be stated. For example:

$3 + 4 = 7$ $a + b = 10$
gives $7 - 4 = 3$ and $7 - 3 = 4$ gives $10 - a = b$ and $10 - b = a$
$3 \times 4 = 12$ $ab = 10$
gives $\dfrac{12}{3} = 4$ and $\dfrac{12}{4} = 3$ gives $\dfrac{10}{a} = b$ and $\dfrac{10}{b} = a$

Exercise 6B

1 In each of the following clouds only two expressions are equal to each other. Write down the equal pair.

a

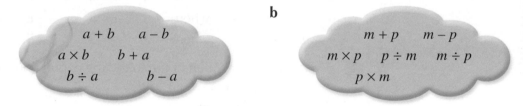

$a + b$ $a - b$
$a \times b$ $b + a$
$b \div a$ $b - a$

b

$m + p$ $m - p$
$m \times p$ $p \div m$ $m \div p$
$p \times m$

2 In each of the following lists, write down all the expressions that equal each other.

a $ab, a + b, b - a, ba, \dfrac{a}{b}, a - b, \dfrac{b}{a}, b + a, a \div b$

b $k \times t, k + t, \dfrac{k}{t}, kt, k \div t, tk, t + k, t \times k, k - t$

3 Write down two more facts that are implied by each of the following statements.

a $a + b = 7$ **b** $ab = 24$ **c** $3 + k = 9$ **d** $\dfrac{8}{a} = 7$

4 Show by the substitution of suitable numbers that:

a $m + n = n + m$ **b** $ab = ba$ **c** $p - t \neq t - p$ **d** $\dfrac{m}{n} \neq \dfrac{n}{m}$

5 Show by the substitution of suitable numbers that:

a $a + b + c = c + b + a$ **b** $acb = abc = cba$

6 Write down the value of each expression when $t = 5$.
a $3t^2$ **b** $(3t)^2$ **c** $4t^2 + 1$ **d** $(4t + 1)^2$

7 If you know that $a + b + c = 180$, write down expressions for $a = \ldots$, $b = \ldots$ and $c = \ldots$.

8 It is known that $abc = 100$. Write down expressions $a = \ldots$, $b = \ldots$ and $c = \ldots$.

9 Show, by substitution, that $3t^2 \neq (3t)^2$.

The following four identities can be used to combine two fractions for the operations of addition, subtraction, multiplication and division.

Addition	Subtraction	Multiplication	Division
$\dfrac{a}{b} + \dfrac{c}{d} = \dfrac{ad + cb}{bd}$	$\dfrac{a}{b} - \dfrac{c}{d} = \dfrac{ad - cb}{bd}$	$\dfrac{a}{b} \times \dfrac{c}{d} = \dfrac{ac}{bd}$	$\dfrac{a}{b} \div \dfrac{c}{d} = \dfrac{ad}{bc}$

For example: $\dfrac{2}{5} + \dfrac{3}{7} = \dfrac{2 \times 7 + 3 \times 5}{5 \times 7} = \dfrac{29}{35}$

and $\dfrac{4}{9} \div \dfrac{1}{3} = \dfrac{4 \times 3}{9 \times 1} = \dfrac{12}{9} = \dfrac{4}{3} = 1\dfrac{1}{3}$

Note that this last example could be cancelled down and made into a mixed number.

Use the identities above to work out the following fraction problems.

Cancel answers down and make into mixed numbers if necessary.

a $\dfrac{1}{4} + \dfrac{3}{5}$ b $\dfrac{2}{3} - \dfrac{2}{7}$ c $\dfrac{2}{5} \times \dfrac{3}{4}$ d $\dfrac{2}{9} + \dfrac{5}{6}$

e $\dfrac{3}{4} + \dfrac{5}{9}$ f $1\dfrac{1}{3} - \dfrac{3}{5}$ g $\dfrac{4}{15} \times \dfrac{5}{8}$ h $1\dfrac{1}{8} \div \dfrac{3}{4}$

Expanding and simplifying expressions

If you add 2 cups to 3 cups, you get 5cups.
In algebra, this can be represented as:

$2c + 3c = 5c$

The terms here are called **like terms**, because they are all multiples of c.

Only like terms can be added or subtracted to simplify an expression. Unlike terms cannot be combined.

Check out these two boxes.

Examples of combining like terms

$3p + 4p = 7p$ $5t + 3t = 8t$

$9w - 4w = 5w$ $12q - 5q = 7q$

$a + 3a + 7a = 11a$

$15m - 2m - m = 12m$

Examples of unlike terms

$x + y$ $2m + 3p$

$7 - 3y$ $5g + 2k$

$m - 3p$

Like terms can be combined even when they are mixed together with unlike terms.
For example:

$2a + p + 4a + 2k = 6a + 2k + p$

Examples of different sorts of like terms mixed together

$4t + 5m + 2m + 3t + m = 7t + 8m$

$5k + 4g - 2k - g = 3k + 3g$

Note: You **never** write the one in front of a variable.

$g = 1g$ $m = 1m$

There are many situations in algebra where there is a need to use brackets in expressions. They keep things tidy! You can **expand** brackets, as shown in Example 6.1. This operation is also called **multiplying out**.

Example 6.1 ▶

Expand and simplify $2(3p + 4) + 3(4p + 1)$.

This means that each term in each pair of brackets is multiplied by the number outside the brackets. This gives:

$2 \times 3p + 2 \times 4 + 3 \times 4p + 3 \times 1$
$= 6p + 8 + 12p + 3$
$= 18p + 11$

Example 6.2 ▶

Expand and simplify $2(3x + 2) - 3(x - 5)$.

Be careful when expanding the second bracket as $-3 \times -5 = +15$.

Expanding gives $6x + 4 - 3x + 15 = 3x + 19$.

Exercise 6C

1 Simplify each of the following expressions.

a $4c + 2c$	**b** $6d + 4d$	**c** $7p - 5p$	**d** $2x + 6x + 3x$
e $4t + 2t - t$	**f** $7m - 3m$	**g** $q + 5q - 2q$	**h** $a + 6a - 3a$
i $4p + p - 2p$	**j** $2w + 3w - w$	**k** $4t + 3t - 5t$	**l** $5g - g - 2g$
ḿ $5x + x + 2x$	**n** $8y - 2y - 3y$	**o** $6f + 3f - 7f$	**p** $8c - 4c - 3c$

2 Simplify each of the following expressions.

a $2x + 2y + 3x + 6y$	**b** $4w + 6t - 2w - 2t$	**c** $4m + 7n + 3m - n$
d $4x + 8y - 2y - 3x$	**e** $8 + 4x - 3 + 2x$	**f** $8p + 9 - 3p - 4$
g $2y + 4x - 3 + x - y$	**h** $5d + 8c - 4c + 7$	**i** $4f + 2 + 3d - 1 - 3f$

3 Expand each of the following expressions.

a $4(x + 5)$	**b** $2(3t + 4)$	**c** $5(3m + 1)$	**d** $4(3w - 2)$
e $6(3m - 4)$	**f** $7(4q - 3)$	**g** $2(3x - 4)$	**h** $3(2t + 7)$
i $7(3k + p - 2)$	**j** $4(3 - k + 2t)$	**k** $5(m - 3 + 6p)$	**l** $4(2 - 5k - 2m)$

4 Expand and simplify each of the following expressions.

a $4(x + 5) + 3(x + 3)$	**b** $5(p + 7) + 3(p + 3)$
c $3(w + 3) + 4(w - 2)$	**d** $6(d + 3) + 3(d - 5)$
e $3(8p + 2) + 3(5p + 1)$	**f** $4(6m + 5) + 2(5m - 4)$
g $5(3w + 7) + 2(2w - 1)$	**h** $7(3c + 2) + 2(5c - 4)$
i $4(t + 6) + 3(4t - 1)$	**j** $5(3x + 2) + 4(3x - 2)$

5 Expand and simplify each of the following expressions.

a $3(x - 4) + 4(x - 6)$	**b** $5(x - 1) - 3(x + 2)$	**c** $4(x + 2) - 2(x - 1)$
d $2(3x - 1) + 2(x - 5)$	**e** $2(4x - 3) - 3(2x + 1)$	**f** $3(2x + 1) - 2(x - 3)$
g $4(x - 3) + 3(2x - 1)$	**h** $2(5x + 6) - 5(2x + 2)$	**i** $3(x - 7) - 3(x - 2)$
j $5(2x + 3) - 2(3x - 6)$		

1   When an expression contains brackets within brackets, first simplify the expression within the innermost brackets.

Expand and simplify each of these.

    a $2[3x + 5(x + 2)]$ **b** $3[4y + 3(2y - 1)]$

    c $4\{m + 2[m + (m - 1)]\}$ **d** $5\{2(t + 1) + 3[4t + 3(2t - 1)]\}$

2   Find at least ten different pairs of brackets which would expand and simplify to give each of the following.

    a $12x + 11y$ **b** $12x - 11y$

Formulae

Where you have a **rule** to calculate some quantity, you can write the rule as a **formula**.

Example 6.3 ▶   A rule to calculate the cost of hiring a hall for a wedding is £200 plus £6 per person. This rule, written as a formula, is:

$$c = 200 + 6n$$

where c = cost in £
          n = number of people

Example 6.4 ▶   Use the formula $c = 200 + 6n$ to calculate the cost of a wedding with 70 people.

Cost = $200 + 6 \times 70 = 200 + 420 = £620$

Exercise 6D

1   Write each of these rules as a formula. Use the first letter of each variable in the formula. (Each letter is printed in **bold**.)

    a   The **c**ost of hiring a boat is £2 per **h**our.

    b   The total **d**istance run each **t**ime 300 metres is run round a track.

    c   **D**ad's age is always **J**oy's age plus 40.

    d   The **c**ost of a party is £50 plus £8 per **p**erson.

    e   The number of bottles of **j**uice needed is 5 plus the number of **p**eople divided by 3.

2   A mechanic uses the formula:

$$c = 8 + 5t$$

where c = cost in £
         t = time, in hours, to complete the work

Calculate what the mechanic charges to complete the work in:

    a 1 hour   **b** 3 hours   **c** 7 hours

3   A singer uses the formula:

$$c = 25 + 15s$$

where c = cost in £
         s = number of songs sung

Calculate what the singer charges to sing the following.

    a 2 songs   **b** 4 songs   **c** 8 songs

(FM) **4** The formula for a child's dose of medicine is:

$$D = \frac{10C - 10}{C}$$

where D = dose, in millilitres, for a child
C = child's age in years

Use the formula to calculate the dose for each of the following ages.

a 8 years **b** 5 years
c $2\frac{1}{2}$ years **d** 10 years

(FM) **5** The formula for the cost of a newspaper advert is:

$$C = 5W + 10A$$

where C = charge in £
W = number of words used
A = area of the advert in cm²

Use the formula to calculate the charge for the following adverts.

a 10 words with an area of 20 cm² **b** 8 words with an area of 6 cm²
c 12 words with an area of 15 cm² **d** 17 words with an area of 15 cm²

(FM) **6** The cost of a badge is given by the formula:

$$C = 60R^2$$

where C = cost in pence
R = radius of badge

Use the formula to calculate the cost of each of these badges.

a Radius 1 cm **b** Radius 2 cm **c** Radius 2.5 cm

Extension **Work**

A three-tier set of number bricks looks like this:

The numbers on two adjacent bricks are added
to create the number on the brick above them.

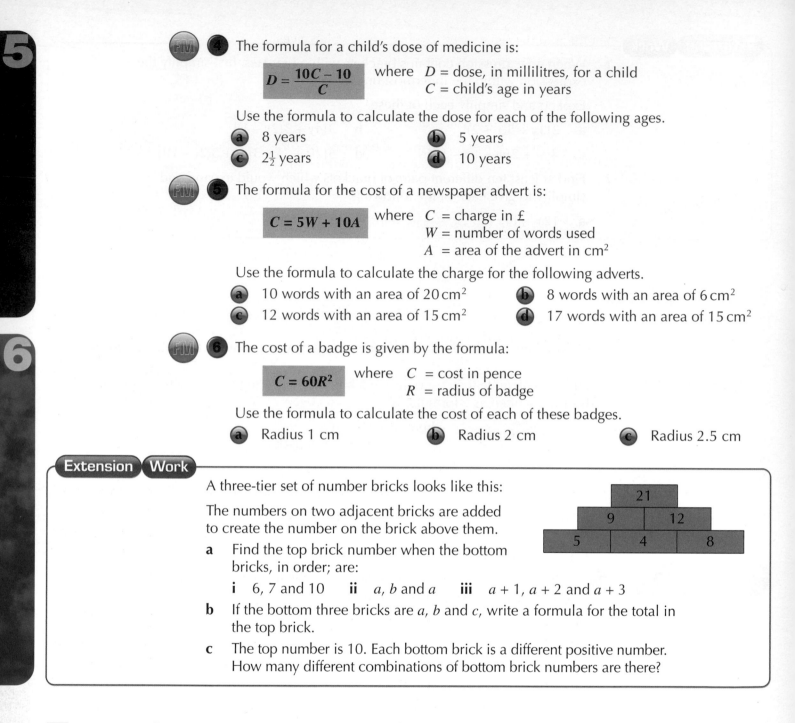

a Find the top brick number when the bottom
bricks, in order; are:

i 6, 7 and 10 **ii** a, b and a **iii** $a + 1$, $a + 2$ and $a + 3$

b If the bottom three bricks are a, b and c, write a formula for the total in
the top brick.

c The top number is 10. Each bottom brick is a different positive number.
How many different combinations of bottom brick numbers are there?

Equations

An equation states that two things are equal.
These can be two expressions or an expression
and a quantity.

An equation can be represented by a pair of scales.
When the scales balance, both sides are equal.

The left-hand pan has 3 bags and 2 marbles.

The right-hand pan has 17 marbles.

Each bag contains the same number of marbles.
How many marbles are in a bag?

Let the number of marbles in a bag be x, which gives: $3x + 2 = 17$

Take 2 marbles away from each side: $3x + 2 - 2 = 17 - 2$

This gives: $3x = 15$

Now, $3x$ means $3 \times x$. This is equal to 15. So: $x = 5$

There are 5 marbles in each bag.

You will usually solve these types of equation by subtracting or adding to both sides in order to have a single term on each side of the equals sign.

Example 6.5 ▷

Solve $4x + 3 = 31$.

Subtract 3 from both sides: $4x + 3 - 3 = 31 - 3$

$$4x = 28$$
$$(4 \times ? = 28)$$
$$x = 7$$

Example 6.6 ▷

Solve $3x - 5 = 13$.

Add 5 to both sides: $3x - 5 + 5 = 13 + 5$

$$3x = 18$$
$$(3 \times ? = 18)$$
$$x = 6$$

Exercise 6E

 Solve each of the following equations.

a	$2x + 3 = 11$	**b**	$2x + 5 = 13$	**c**	$3x + 4 = 19$	**d**	$3x + 7 = 19$
e	$4m + 1 = 21$	**f**	$5k + 6 = 21$	**g**	$4n + 9 = 17$	**h**	$2x + 7 = 27$
i	$6h + 5 = 23$	**j**	$3t + 5 = 26$	**k**	$8x + 3 = 35$	**l**	$5y + 3 = 28$
m	$7x + 3 = 10$	**n**	$4t + 7 = 39$	**o**	$3x + 8 = 20$	**p**	$8m + 5 = 21$

2 Solve each of the following equations.

a	$3x - 2 = 13$	**b**	$2m - 5 = 1$	**c**	$4x - 1 = 11$	**d**	$5t - 3 = 17$
e	$2x - 3 = 13$	**f**	$4m - 5 = 19$	**g**	$3m - 2 = 10$	**h**	$7x - 3 = 25$
i	$5m - 2 = 18$	**j**	$3k - 4 = 5$	**k**	$8x - 5 = 11$	**l**	$2t - 3 = 7$
m	$4x - 3 = 5$	**n**	$8y - 3 = 29$	**o**	$5x - 4 = 11$	**p**	$3m - 1 = 17$

3 Solve each of the following equations.

a	$2x + 3 = 11$	**b**	$3x + 4 = 10$	**c**	$5x - 1 = 29$	**d**	$4x - 3 = 25$
e	$3m - 2 = 13$	**f**	$5m + 4 = 49$	**g**	$7m + 3 = 24$	**h**	$4m - 5 = 23$
i	$6k + 1 = 25$	**j**	$5k - 3 = 2$	**k**	$3k - 1 = 23$	**l**	$2k + 5 = 15$
m	$7x - 3 = 18$	**n**	$4x + 3 = 43$	**o**	$5x + 6 = 31$	**p**	$9x - 4 = 68$

 The solution of each of the following equations may involve a decimal or a fraction.

a	$2x + 7 = 8$	**b**	$5x + 3 = 4$	**c**	$2x + 3 = 8$	**d**	$4x + 7 = 20$
e	$5x - 3 = 9$	**f**	$2x - 7 = 10$	**g**	$4x - 5 = 6$	**h**	$10x - 3 = 8$

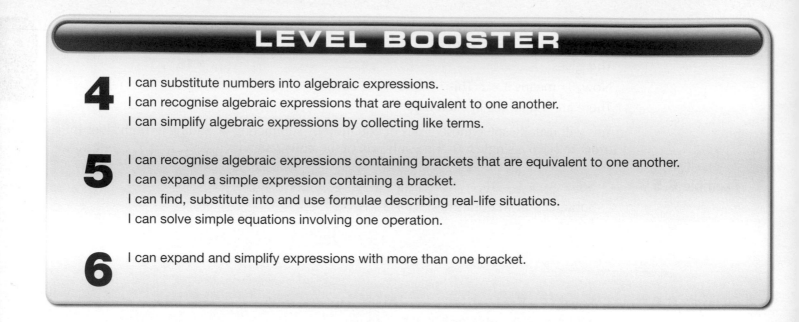

4
I can substitute numbers into algebraic expressions.
I can recognise algebraic expressions that are equivalent to one another.
I can simplify algebraic expressions by collecting like terms.

5
I can recognise algebraic expressions containing brackets that are equivalent to one another.
I can expand a simple expression containing a bracket.
I can find, substitute into and use formulae describing real-life situations.
I can solve simple equations involving one operation.

6
I can expand and simplify expressions with more than one bracket.

National Test questions

1 *2002 Paper 1*

a When $x = 5$, work out the values of the expressions below.

$2x + 13 =$

$5x - 5 =$

$3 + 6x =$

b When $2y + 11 = 17$, work out the value of y.

Show your working.

2 *2004 Paper 2*

Shoe sizes in Britain and Germany are different.

The rule below shows how to change a British shoe size to a German shoe size.

> **Multiply** the British shoe size by **1.25**,
> then **add 32**, then **round** the answer to
> the nearest whole number

Tom's British shoe size is **7**, Karl's British shoe size is $7\frac{1}{2}$

They say:

'The rule shows that we have the same **German** shoe size.'

Are they correct? Write down Yes or No.

Show working to explain your answer.

3   *2005 Paper 1*

Solve these equations.

$3y + 1 = 16$ $y = \ldots$

$18 = 4k + 6$ $k = \ldots$

Skiing trip

Use the information in the key to answer the following questions.

On-line Ski Hire Prices

- Minimum rental 2 days.
- Prices shown are for 2 days' and 8 days' hire.
- Prices include boots.
- All other days are pro-rata.
- 20% deposit required when ordering.

ADULTS	2 days	8 days
Platinum Saloman Crossmax W12 – or equivalent	€52.32	€192.72
Gold Rossignol Radical 8S ou 8X Oversize – or equivalent	€46.72	€171.94
Silver Saloman Aero RT– or equivalent	€37.60	€138.40
CHILDREN	2 days	8 days
Junior Surf Dynastar Starlett Teen– or equivalent	€26.56	€97.84
Junior Ski Saloman X-wing fury Junior– or equivalent	€16.16	€59.42
Kid Dynastar My First Dynastar– or equivalent	€12.16	€44.74

1 Mr Khan, Mrs Khan, their son Rafiq and their daughter Sufia hire skis for 8 days. Mr Khan hires a pair of Saloman Crossmax W12, Mrs Khan hires a pair of Saloman Aero RT, Rafiq hires a pair of Dynastar Starlett Teen and Sufia hires a pair of Saloman X-wing Fury Junior. What is their total bill?

2 The hire company allows a 10% discount per person for groups of 8 or more people. A party of 12 friends take a skiing trip. They all go for the Adult 'Platinum' deal for 8 days.

   a What is the cost of this deal for one person with the discount?

   b How much will the 12 friends pay altogether?

3

a Explain why the extra daily rate for the Adult 'Gold' deal is €20.87.

b Explain why 6 days' hire for the Adult 'Gold' deal would cost €130.20.

Work out the cost of:

c 10 days' hire for the 'Platinum' deal

d 5 days' hire for the Junior Surf deal.

4 Mr Smith hires some Saloman Crossmax W12 skis for 8 days. He pays £50 as a deposit. The exchange rate is £1 = €1.38. When he pays the balance, the exchange rate has changed to £1 = €1.42. How much will he pay in pounds? Answer to the nearest pound.

5 Colne Valley High School take a party skiing for 6 days. The bill for ski hire is shown below. Complete the bill.

Invoice for Colne Valley

Number of rentals	Type of ski	Rate	Total cost
11	Junior Surf		
9	Junior Ski		
10	Kid		
3	Platinum		
2	Gold	130.20	
	Total hire cost		
	Less 10% discount		
	Less £600 deposit @ 1.42		
Total less discount and deposit			

This chapter is going to show you
- The vocabulary and notation for lines and angles
- How to identify alternate and corresponding angles
- How to use angles at a point, angles on a straight line, angles in a triangle and in a quadrilateral, and vertically opposite angles
- How to use coordinates in all four quadrants

What you should already know
- The geometric properties of triangles and quadrilaterals
- How to plot coordinates in the first quadrant

Lines and angles

Lines   A straight line can be considered to have infinite length.

A **line segment** has finite length.

A ——————————————————————— B

The line segment AB has two end points, one at A and the other at B.

Two lines lie in a **plane**, which is a flat surface.

Two lines either are parallel or intersect.

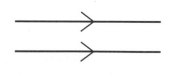

Parallel lines never meet.

These two lines **intersect** at a point X.

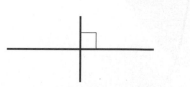

These two lines intersect at right angles. The lines are said to be **perpendicular**.

Angles   When two lines meet at a point, they form an **angle**. An angle is a measure of rotation and is measured in degrees (°).

Types of angle

Right angle
90°

Half turn
180°

Full turn
360°

Acute angle
less than 90°

Obtuse angle
between 90° and 180°

Reflex angle
between 180° and 360°

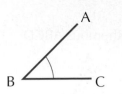

Describing angles

The angle at B can be written as:

∠B or ∠ABC or AB̂C

Describing triangles

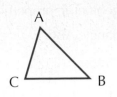

The triangle can be represented by △ABC. It has three vertices A, B and C; three angles, ∠A, ∠B and ∠C; three sides, AB, AC and BC.

Example 7.1 ▷

Describe the geometric properties of these two shapes.

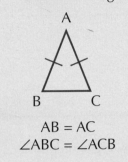

a Isosceles triangle ABC

AB = AC
∠ABC = ∠ACB

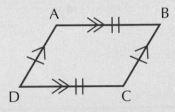

b Parallelogram ABCD

AB = CD and AD = BC
AB is parallel to CD or AB // CD
AD is parallel to BC or AD // BC

Corresponding and alternate angles

A line which intersects a set of parallel lines is called a **transversal**.

Notice in the diagram that eight distinct angles are formed by a transversal which intersects a pair of parallel lines.

The two angles marked on the diagram above are equal and are called **corresponding angles**.

Look for the letter F to identify corresponding angles.

The two angles marked on the diagram above are equal and are called **alternate angles**.

Look for the letter Z to identify alternate angles.

Exercise 7A

1 Write down which of the angles below are acute, which are obtuse and which are reflex. Estimate the size of each one.

a   **b**   **c**   **d**   **e**   **f**

2 For the shape ABCDE:

  a Write down two lines that are equal in length.

  b Write down two lines that are parallel.

  c Write down two lines that are perpendicular to each other.

  d Copy the diagram and draw on the two diagonals BD and CE. What do you notice about the two diagonals?

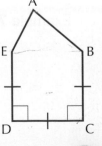

6

3 Write down the geometric properties of these three shapes.

a Equilateral triangle ABC   **b** Square ABCD   **c** Rhombus ABCD

4

Copy and complete each of the following sentences:

a   *a* and … are corresponding angles   **b**   *b* and … are corresponding angles

c   *c* and … are corresponding angles   **d**   *d* and … are corresponding angles

e   *e* and … are alternate angles   **f**   *f* and … are alternate angles

g   *k* and … are corresponding angles   **h**   *u* and … are corresponding angles

i   *l* and … are corresponding angles   **j**   *r* and … are corresponding angles

k   *n* and … are alternate angles   **l**   *s* and … are alternate angles

---

Extension **Work**

1 For the regular hexagon ABCDEF:

     a Write down all the pairs of sides that are parallel.

     b Write down all the diagonals that are perpendicular.

2 Cut the rectangle ABCD into two parts with one straight cut. How many different shapes can you make? Draw a diagram to show each different cut you use.

Calculating angles

You can calculate the **unknown angles** in a diagram from the information given. Unknown angles are usually denoted by letters, such as *a*, *b*, *c*, … .

Remember: usually the diagrams are not to scale.

Angles around a point

Angles around a point add up to 360°.

Example 7.2 ▷

Calculate the size of the angle *a*.

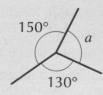

$a = 360° - 150° - 130°$

$a = 80°$

Angles on a straight line

Angles on a straight line add up to 180°.

Example 7.3 ▷

Calculate the size of the angle *b*.

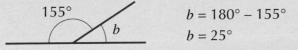

$b = 180° - 155°$

$b = 25°$

Angles in a triangle

The angles in a triangle add up to 180°.

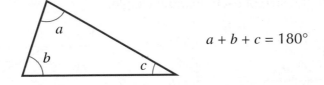

$a + b + c = 180°$

Example 7.4 ▷

Calculate the size of the angle *c*.

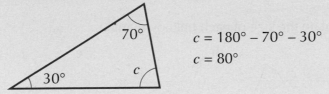

$c = 180° - 70° - 30°$

$c = 80°$

Angles in a quadrilateral

The angles in a quadrilateral add up to 360°.

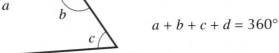

$a + b + c + d = 360°$

Example 7.5 ▷

Calculate the size of angle *d*.

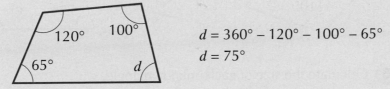

$d = 360° - 120° - 100° - 65°$

$d = 75°$

Vertically opposite angles

When two lines intersect, the opposite angles are equal.

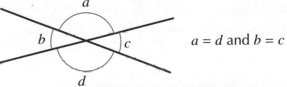

$a = d$ and $b = c$

Example 7.6 ▷

Calculate the sizes of angles *e* and *f*.

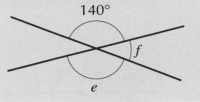

$e = 140°$ (opposite angles)

$f = 40°$ (angles on a straight line)

Exercise 7B

1 Calculate the size of each unknown angle.

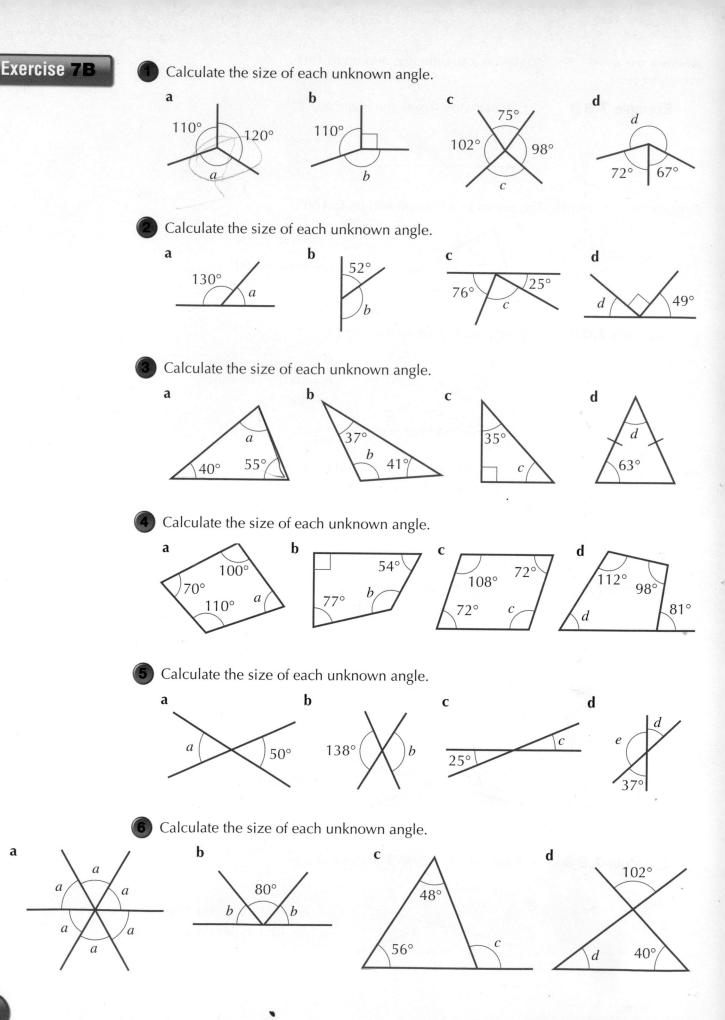

a

110° 120°
a

b

110°
b

c

75°
102° 98°
c

d

d
72° 67°

2 Calculate the size of each unknown angle.

a

130°
a

b

52°
b

c

76° 25°
c

d

d 49°

3 Calculate the size of each unknown angle.

a

a
40° 55°

b

37°
b 41°

c

35°
c

d

d
63°

4 Calculate the size of each unknown angle.

a

100°
70°
110° *a*

b

54°
77° *b*

c

72°
108°
72° *c*

d

112° 98°
d 81°

5 Calculate the size of each unknown angle.

a

a 50°

b

138° *b*

c

c
25°

d

d
e
37°

6 Calculate the size of each unknown angle.

a

a
a *a*
a *a*
a

b

80°
b *b*

c

48°
56° *c*

d

102°
d 40°

7 Geometrical proofs

a Copy the following two proofs and then write them out without looking at the answers.

i The sum of the angles of a triangle is 180°.

To prove $a + b + c = 180°$.

Draw a line parallel to one side of the triangle.
$x = b$ (alternate angles)
$y = c$ (alternate angles)
$a + x + y = 180°$ (angles on a straight line)

So, $a + b + c = 180°$.

ii An exterior angle of a triangle is equal to the sum of the two interior opposite angles.

x is an exterior angle of the triangle.
To prove $a + b = x$.

$a + b + c = 180°$ (angles in a triangle)
$x + c = 180°$ (angles on a straight line)

So, $a + b = x$.

b Write out a proof that the sum of the angles of a quadrilateral is 360°. (Hint: Divide the quadrilateral into two triangles.)

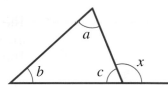

Extension Work

1 Calculate the size of each unknown angle.

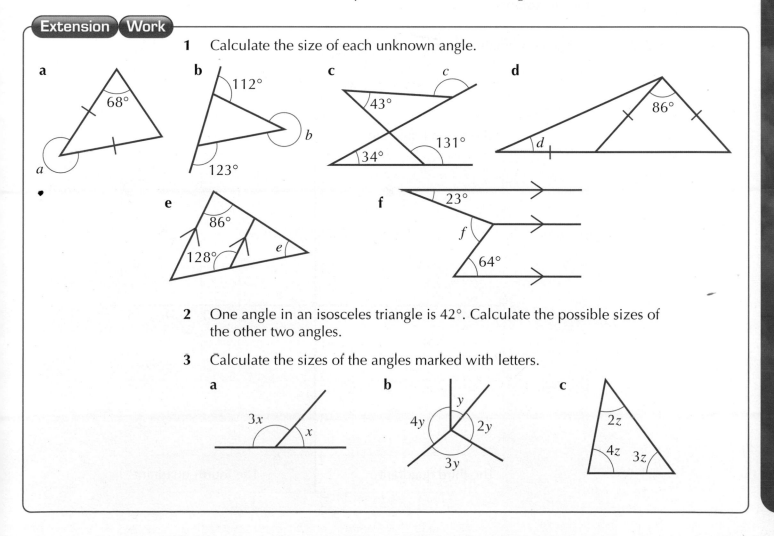

a 68°

b 112° 123° *b*

c *c* 43° 34° 131°

d 86° *d*

e 86° 128° *e*

f 23° *f* 64°

2 One angle in an isosceles triangle is 42°. Calculate the possible sizes of the other two angles.

3 Calculate the sizes of the angles marked with letters.

a 3x x

b 4y y 2y 3y

c 2z 4z 3z

95

Coordinates

We use **coordinates** to locate a point on a grid.

The grid consists of two axes, called the **x-axis** and the **y-axis**. They are perpendicular to each other.

The two axes meet at a point called the **origin**, which is labelled O.

The point A on the grid is 4 units across and 3 units up.

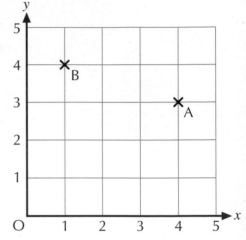

We say that the coordinates of A are (4, 3), which is usually written as A(4, 3).

The first number, 4, is the *x*-coordinate of A and the second number, 3, is the *y*-coordinate of A. The *x*-coordinate is *always* written first.

When plotting a point on a grid, a ✗ or a ● is usually used.

The coordinates of the origin are (0, 0) and the coordinates of the point B are (1, 4).

The grid system can be extended to negative numbers and points can be plotted in all **four quadrants**.

Example 7.7 ▶ The coordinates of the points on the grid are:

A(4, 2), B(–2, 3), C(–3, –1), D(1, –4)

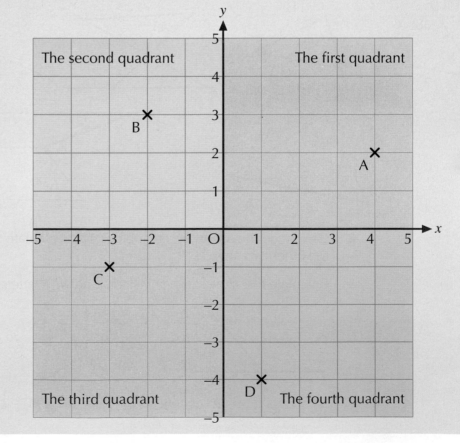

1 Write down the coordinates of the points P, Q, R, S and T.

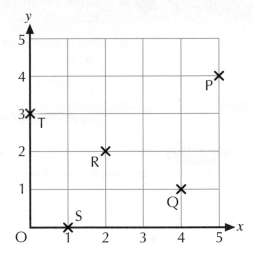

2 **a** Make a copy of the grid in Question 1. Then plot the points A(1, 1), B(1, 5) and C(4, 5).

   b The three points are the vertices of a rectangle. Plot point D to complete the rectangle.

   c Write down the coordinates of D.

3 Write down the coordinates of the points A, B, C, D, E, F, G and H.

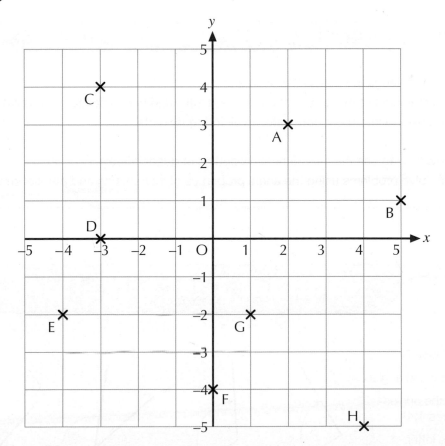

4 **a** Make a copy of the grid in Question 3. Then plot the points A(−4, 3), B(−2, −2), C(0, 1), D(2, −2) and E(4, 3).

   b Join the points in the order given. What letter have you drawn?

5
a Make a copy of the grid in Question 3. Then plot the points W(3, 4), X(3, –2) and Y(–3, –2).

b The points form three vertices of a square WXYZ. Plot the point Z and draw the square.

c What are the coordinates of the point Z?

d Draw in the diagonals of the square. What are the coordinates of the point of intersection of the diagonals?

Extension Work

Coordinates and lines

- Draw on a grid *x*-and *y*-axes from –8 to 8.
- Plot the points (0, 2) and (6, 8) and join them to make a straight line.
- Write down the coordinates of other points that lie on the line.
- Can you spot a rule that connects the *x*-coordinate and the *y*-coordinate?
- Extend the line into the third quadrant. Does your rule still work?
- The rule you have found is given by the formula $y = x + 2$.
- Now draw the following lines on different grids using these formulae:

  a $y = x + 3$ **b** $y = x$ **c** $y = x - 2$

LEVEL BOOSTER

5
I know the language associated with angles.
I know the sum of the angles of a triangle is 180° and the angles round a point is 360°.
I can use and interpret coordinates in all four quadrants.

6
I know how to use the geometrical properties of quadrilaterals.
I can solve problems using the angle properties of intersecting and parallel straight lines.

National Test questions

1 *2000 Paper 1*

Look at these angles.

One of the angles measures 120°.

Write its letter.

Angle P   Angle Q   Angle R   Angle S   Angle T

2 *2005 4–6 Paper 1*

The diagram shows triangle PQR.

Work out the sizes of angles a, b and c.

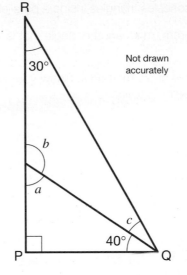

Not drawn accurately

3 *2006 Paper 2*

Look at the diagram, made from four straight lines.

The lines marked with arrows are parallel.

Work out the sizes of the angles marked with letters.

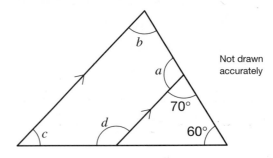

Not drawn accurately

4 *2003 Paper 1*

The drawing shows how shapes A and B fit together to make a **right-angled** triangle.

Work out the size of each of the angles in shape B.

Write them in the correct place in a copy of shape B below.

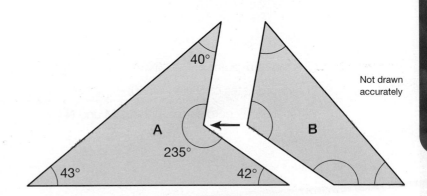

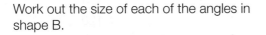

Not drawn accurately

5 *2001 Paper 1*

The diagram shows two isosceles triangles inside a parallelogram.

a On a copy of the diagram, mark another angle that is 75°. Label it 75°.

b Calculate the size of the angle marked k. Show your working.

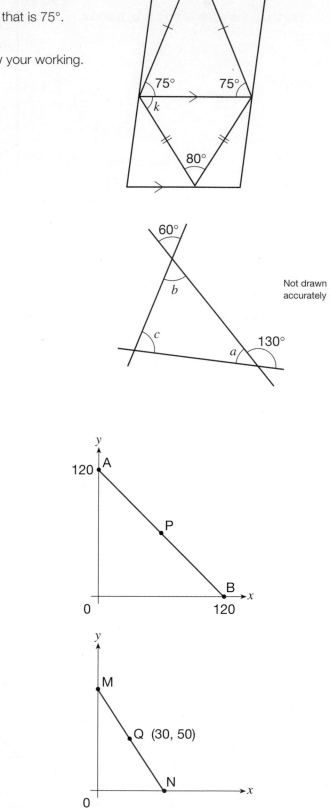

6 *2007 Paper 1*

The diagram shows three straight lines.

Work out the sizes of angles a, b and c

Give reasons for your answers.

$a = ...$° because ... $b = ...$° because ...

$c = ...$° because ...

Not drawn accurately

7 *2005 Paper 1*

a P is the **mid-point** of line AB.

What are the coordinates of point **P**?

b Q is the **mid-point** of line MN.

The coordinates of Q are (30, 50)

What are the coordinates of points **M** and **N**?

This chapter is going to show you

- How to collect and organise discrete and continuous data
- How to create data collection forms
- How to create questionnaires
- How to use frequency tables to collate discrete and continuous data
- How to conduct surveys and experiments
- How to draw simple conclusions from data

What you should a

- How to create a tally c
- How to draw bar charts a pictograms

Using a tally chart

Discrete data

What method of transport do pupils use to travel to school?

When pupils are asked this question, they will give different methods of travelling, such as bus, car, bike, walking, train and even some others we don't yet know about!

A good way to collect this data is to fill in a tally chart as each pupil is asked how he or she travels to school. For example:

Type of transport	Tally	Frequency
Bus	⊬⊬⊬ IIII	9
Car	⊬⊬⊬	5
Bike	II	2
Walking	⊬⊬⊬ ⊬⊬⊬ IIII	14
Other		
	Total	30

This sort of data is called **discrete data** because there is only a fixed number of possible answers.

How far do you travel to school?

Because pupils could give any answer within a reasonable range, such as 2 miles, 1.3 miles, 1.25 miles, we say that the data is **continuous**. As all the data may be different, a good way to collect this data is to group it into distance intervals.

For example, we use 2 < Distance ≤ 4 to mean the distance is more than 2 miles and less than or equal to 4 miles. So, we include 4 miles but not 2 miles in this category.

Distance to travel to school (miles)	Tally	Frequency
0 < Distance ≤ 2	┼┼┼┼ I I	7
2 < Distance ≤ 4	I I I I	4
4 < Distance ≤ 6	I I I	3
6 < Distance ≤ 8	┼┼┼┼ ┼┼┼┼ I I I	13
	Total	27

Exercise 8A

1 Use your own class tally sheet (or the one on page 101) to draw a chart illustrating the methods of transport used by pupils to get to school.

2 Use your own class tally sheet (or the one above) to draw a chart illustrating the distance that pupils travel to school.

Extension Work

Put into a spreadsheet the data from one of the tally charts in this lesson.
Then create the statistical charts available. Pay close attention to the labelling.

Using the correct data

Do certain newspapers use more long words than the other newspapers?

There are many different newspapers about. Can you list six different national newspapers?

Now consider Ted's question. The strict way to answer this would be to count, in each newspaper, all the words and all their letters. But this would take too long, so we take what is called a **sample**. We count, say, 100 words from each newspaper to find the length of each word.

Exercise 8B

This whole exercise is a class activity.

1 **a** You will be given either a whole newspaper or a page from one.
b Create a data capture form (a tally chart) like the one below.

Number of letters	Tally	Frequency
1		
2		
3		
4		
5		

c Choose a typical page from the newspaper. Then select at least two different articles. Next, count the number of letters in each word from each article (or paragraph), and fill in the tally chart. Do not miss out any words. Before you start to count, see part **f** below.

d Decide what to do with such things as:
  Numbers – 6 would count as 1, six would count as 3.
  Hyphenated words – Ignore the hyphen.
  Abbreviations – Just count the letters that are there.

e Once you have completed this task, fill in the frequency column. Now create a bar chart of the results.

f Each of you will have taken a different newspaper. So what about comparing your results with others'? To do this, you must all use the same number of words.

Look at the following misleading conclusions that arise from not using like data.

Travelling to school Two different classes did a survey of how pupils travelled to school.

They both made pie charts to show their results.

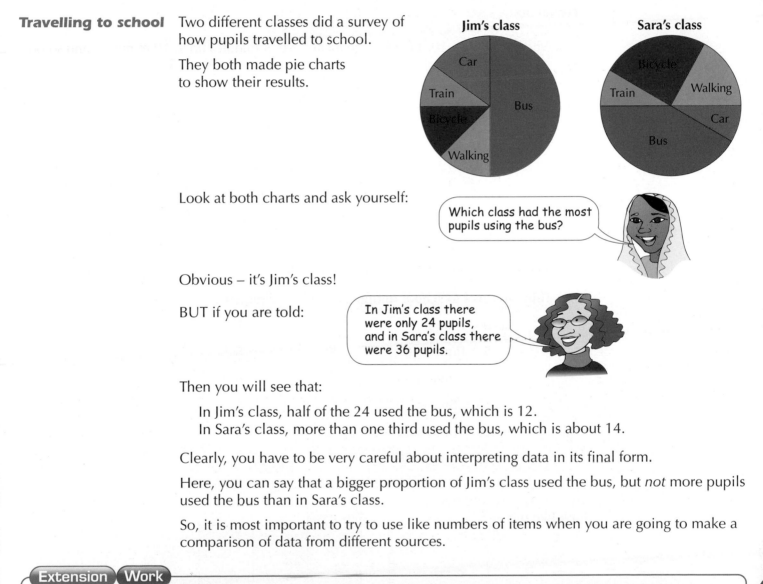

Look at both charts and ask yourself:

> Which class had the most pupils using the bus?

Obvious – it's Jim's class!

BUT if you are told:

> In Jim's class there were only 24 pupils, and in Sara's class there were 36 pupils.

Then you will see that:

  In Jim's class, half of the 24 used the bus, which is 12.
  In Sara's class, more than one third used the bus, which is about 14.

Clearly, you have to be very careful about interpreting data in its final form.

Here, you can say that a bigger proportion of Jim's class used the bus, but *not* more pupils used the bus than in Sara's class.

So, it is most important to try to use like numbers of items when you are going to make a comparison of data from different sources.

Extension **Work**

Now go back to the newspaper articles and use continuous data. For example, you could ask pupils in your class, and in other classes, to read the sample of 100 words and time them to see if the papers with longer words take any longer to read. Write a short report of your findings.

6

Grouped frequencies

How long does it take you to get to school in the morning?

A class was asked this question and the replies, in minutes, were:

6 min, 3 min, 5 min, 20 min, 15 min, 11 min, 13 min, 28 min, 30 min, 5 min, 2 min, 6 min, 8 min, 18 min, 23 min, 22 min, 17 min, 13 min, 4 min, 2 min, 30 min, 17 min, 19 min, 25 min, 8 min, 3 min, 9 min, 12 min, 15 min, 8 min

There are too many different values here to make a sensible bar chart. So we group them to produce a **grouped frequency table**, as shown below. The different groups the data has been put into are called **classes**. Where possible, classes are kept the same size as each other.

Time (minutes)	0–5	6–10	11–15	16–20	21–25	26–30
Frequency	7	6	6	5	3	3

Notice how we use 6–10, 11–15, … to mean 'over 5 minutes up to 10 minutes', and so on.

A frequency diagram has been drawn from this data, and information put on each bar about the method of transport.

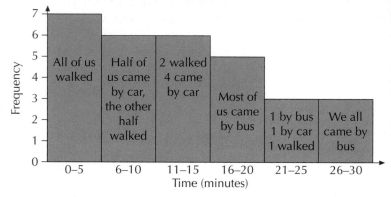

We could also use a continuous scale for this data.

Time to travel to school (minutes)	Frequency
0 < Time ≤ 5	7
5 < Time ≤ 10	6
10 < Time ≤ 15	6
15 < Time ≤ 20	5
20 < Time ≤ 25	3
25 < Time ≤ 30	3

The diagram would now look like this.

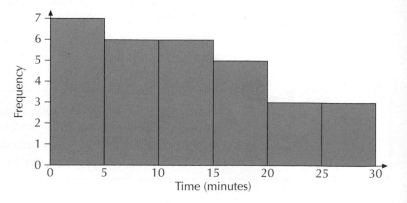

Exercise 8C

1 A class did a survey on how many pencils each pupil had with them in school. The results of this survey are:

4, 7, 2, 18, 1, 16, 19, 15, 13, 0, 9, 17, 4, 6, 10, 12, 15, 8, 3, 14, 19, 14, 15, 18, 5, 16, 3, 6, 5, 18, 12

a Put this data into a grouped frequency table with a class size of 5: that is, 0–4, 5–9, 10–14 …

b Draw a frequency diagram from the data.

2 A teacher asked her class: 'How many hours a week do you spend on a computer?'

She asked them to give an average, rounded figure in hours. This was their response:

3, 6, 9, 2, 23, 18, 6, 8, 29, 27, 2, 1, 0, 5, 19, 23, 20, 21, 7, 4, 23, 8, 7, 1, 0, 25, 24, 8, 13, 18, 15, 16

These are some of the reasons pupils gave for the length of time they spent on a computer:

'I haven't got one.' 'I play games on mine.' 'I always try to do my homework on the computer.' 'I can't use it when I want to, because my brother's always on it.'

a Put the above data into a grouped frequency table with a class size of five.

b Draw a frequency diagram with the information. Try to include in the chart the reasons given.

3 Use the data you have from your survey on the number of letters in words to create a grouped frequency table:

a with a class size of three   **b** with a class size of five

c Which class size seems most sensible to use in this case?

4 The table shows the times of goals scored in football matches played on one weekend in November.

Time of goals (minutes)	Frequency
$0 < \text{Time} \leq 15$	3
$15 < \text{Time} \leq 30$	6
$30 < \text{Time} \leq 45$	8
$45 < \text{Time} \leq 60$	4
$60 < \text{Time} \leq 75$	2
$75 < \text{Time} \leq 90$	5

a One goal was scored after exactly 75 minutes. In which class was it recorded?

b Five teams scored in the last five minutes of their games. Write down what other information this tells you.

c Draw a frequency diagram to represent the data in the table.

Extension Work

Collect data about the heights of the pupils in your class. Design a frequency table to record the information. Draw a frequency diagram from your table of results. Comment on your results.

Data collection

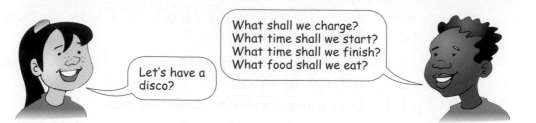

Let's ask a sample of the pupils in our school these questions. In other words, not everyone, but a few from each group.

You ask each question, then immediately complete your data collection form.

An example of a suitable data collection form is shown below.

Year group	Boy or girl	How much to charge?	Time to start?	Time to finish?	What would you like to eat?
Y7	B	£1	7 pm	11 pm	Crisps, beefburgers, chips
Y7	G	50p	7 pm	9 pm	Chips, crisps, lollies
Y8	G	£2	7.30 pm	10 pm	Crisps, hot dogs
Y11	B	£3	8.30 pm	11.30 pm	Chocolate, pizza

Keep track of the age	Try to ask equal numbers	Once the data is collected, it can be sorted into frequency tables.

There are five stages in running this type of survey:
- Deciding what questions to ask and who to ask.
- Creating a simple, suitable data collection form for all the questions.
- Asking the questions and completing the data collection form.
- After collecting all the data, collating it in frequency tables.
- Analysing the data to draw conclusions from the survey.

The size of your sample will depend on many things. It may be simply the first 50 people you come across. Or you may want 10% of the available people.

In the above example, a good sample would probably be about four from each class, two boys and two girls.

Exercise 8D

A class did the above survey on a sample of 10 pupils from each of the Key Stage 3 years. Their data collection chart is shown on the next page.

1. a   Create the frequency tables for the suggested charges from each year group Y7, Y8 and Y9.

    b   Comment on the differences between the year groups.

2. a   Create the frequency tables for the suggested starting times from each year group Y7, Y8 and Y9.

    b   Comment on the differences between the year groups.

3 **a** Create the frequency tables for the suggested lengths of time the disco should last from each year group Y7, Y8 and Y9.

b Comment on the differences between the year groups.

Data Collection Chart

Year group	Boy or girl	How much to charge	Time to start	Time to finish	What would you like to eat?
Y7	B	£1	7 pm	11 pm	Crisps, beefburgers, chips
Y7	G	50p	7 pm	9 pm	Chips, crisps, lollies
Y8	G	£2	7.30 pm	10 pm	Crisps, hot dogs
Y9	B	£3	8.30 pm	11.30 pm	Chocolate, pizza
Y9	G	£2	8 pm	10 pm	Pizza
Y9	B	£2.50	7.30 pm	9.30 pm	Hot dogs, Chocolate
Y8	G	£1	8 pm	10.30 pm	Crisps
Y7	B	75p	7 pm	9 pm	Crisps, beefburgers
Y7	B	£1	7.30 pm	10.30 pm	Crisps, lollies
Y8	B	£1.50	7 pm	9 pm	Crisps, chips, hot dogs
Y9	G	£2	8 pm	11 pm	Pizza, chocolate
Y9	G	£1.50	8 pm	10.30 pm	Chips, pizza
Y9	G	£2	8 pm	11 pm	Crisps, pizza
Y7	G	£1.50	7 pm	9 pm	Crisps, lollies, chocolate
Y8	B	£2	7.30 pm	9.30 pm	Crisps, lollies, chocolate
Y8	B	£1	8 pm	10 pm	Chips, hot dogs
Y9	B	£1.50	8 pm	11 pm	Pizza
Y7	B	50p	7 pm	9.30 pm	Crisps, hot dogs
Y8	G	75p	8 pm	10.30 pm	Crisps, chips
Y9	B	£2	7.30 pm	10.30 pm	Pizza
Y8	G	£1.50	7.30 pm	10 pm	Chips, hot dogs, chocolate
Y8	B	£1.25	7 pm	9.30 pm	Chips, hot dogs, lollies
Y9	G	£3	7 pm	9.30 pm	Crisps, pizza
Y9	B	£2.50	8 pm	10.30 pm	Crisps, hot dogs
Y7	G	25p	7.30 pm	10 pm	Crisps, beefburgers, lollies
Y7	G	50p	7 pm	9 pm	Crisps, pizza
Y7	G	£1	7 pm	9.30 pm	Crisps, pizza
Y8	B	£2	8 pm	10 pm	Crisps, chips, chocolate
Y8	G	£1.50	7.30 pm	9.30 pm	Chips, beefburgers
Y7	B	£1	7.30 pm	10 pm	Crisps, lollies

5
I can compare two simple distributions.
I can interpret graphs and diagrams, drawing conclusions.

6
I can collect and record continuous data, choosing appropriate equal class intervals for frequency tables.
I can construct and interpret frequency diagrams.

National Test questions

1 *2006 Paper 2*

Wine gums are sweets that are made in different colours.

Pupils tested whether people can taste the difference between black wine gums and other wine gums.

The percentage bar charts show three pupils' results.

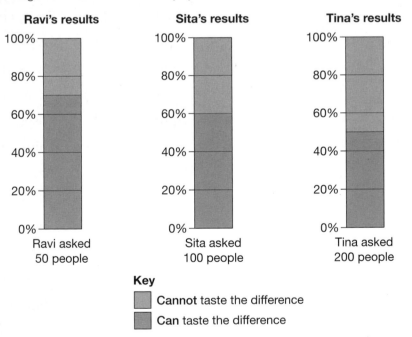

Ravi's results

Ravi asked
50 people

Sita's results

Sita asked
100 people

Tina's results

Tina asked
200 people

Key

Cannot taste the difference

Can taste the difference

a Copy and complete this table.

	Number of people who were tested	Number of people who can taste the difference	Number of people who cannot taste the difference
Ravi	50		
Sita	100		
Tina	200		

b Explain why **Tina's** results are likely to be **more reliable** than Ravi's or Sita's.

2 *2001 Paper 1*

The diagrams show the number of hours of sunshine in two different months.

a How many days are there in month A?

28, 29, 30, 31 or not possible to tell

b How many days are there in month B?

28, 29, 30, 31 or not possible to tell

c Which month had more hours of sunshine?

Month A or Month B

Explain how you know.

Number of hours of sunshine in month A

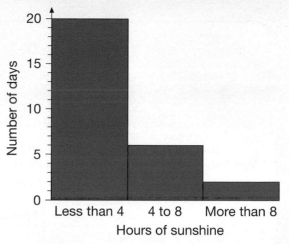

Number of hours of sunshine in month B

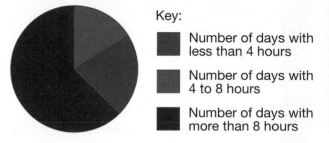

3 *2007 Paper 2*

In a survey, 60 people were asked:

What kind of newspaper did you buy today?

Here are the results.

Type of newspaper	Number of people
Morning newspaper	35
Evening newspaper	10
No newspaper	15

Copy and complete the pie chart to show this information, using a radius of 5 cm.

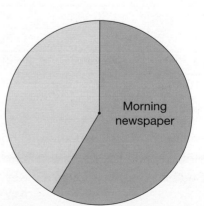

Be a school chef for a day

1 Your class has been asked to transform the school canteen with the help of a professional chef. In order to develop your menu with him, you need to collect certain data before presenting your findings and trialling recipes. The tally chart below shows pupils' choices for food.

	Key Stage 3	Frequency		Key Stage 4	Frequency
Pasta	HH		Pasta	HH HH III	
Salad	II		Salad	IIII	
Pizza	HH HH I		Pizza	HH I	
Jacket potato	HH		Jacket potato	HH IIII	
Curry	HH HH		Curry	HH HH IIII	
Toasties	HH I		Toasties	HH HH I	

a Draw a dual bar chart to illustrate the differences between the two key stages.

b Are there any choices that you would probably consider not offering?

Explain your answer.

2 You now have to work out how your menu will be priced with the chef. In order to do this you need to know how much pupils will be prepared to pay for lunch each day.

Price	under £1	£1–£2	over £2
Y7	30	45	12
Y8	25	50	18
Y9	18	42	25
Y10	11	52	27
Y11	8	55	22

a Draw a multiple bar chart showing how the different year groups voted for the different prices.

b i Combine the year groups as: Key Stage 3 (Y7, Y8 and Y9)
Key Stage 4 (Y10 and Y11)

ii Draw a dual bar chart to illustrate the differences between the two key stages.

3 The table below shows the ingredients needed for the chef to create enough of the particular dish for 50 pupils.

Ingredients needed	Tomato & chicken pasta	Spicy Mexican wraps	Chilli jacket potatoes	Pitta pizza
Chopped tomatoes (tins)	20	0	5	0
Mushrooms (punnets)	5	0	2	2
Peppers (×3)	5	10	2	8
Onions (×5)	6	5	5	3
Potatoes (5 kg bags)	0	0	3	0

Chef wanted to create the following dishes on one day:

Tomato & chicken pasta	for 225 pupils
Spicy Mexican wraps	for 75 pupils
Chilli jacket potatoes	for 275 pupils
Pitta pizza	for 125 pupils

Write down the total numbers required of each ingredient.

This chapter is going to show you

- How to round off positive whole numbers and decimals
- The order of operations
- How to multiply and divide a three-digit whole number by a two-digit whole number without a calculator
- How to use a calculator efficiently

What you should already know

- Tables up to 10 times 10
- Place value of the digits in a number such as 23.508

Rounding

What is wrong with this picture?

It shows that the woman's weight (60 kg) balances the man's weight (110 kg) when both weights are rounded to the nearest 100 kg!

This example highlights the need to round numbers *sensibly*, depending on the situation in which they occur.

But, we do not always need numbers to be precise, and it is easier to work with numbers that are rounded off.

Example 9.1 ▶ Round off each of these numbers to: **i** the nearest 10 **ii** the nearest 100 **iii** the nearest 1000.

a 937	**b** 2363	**c** 3799	**d** 281

a 937 is 940 to the nearest 10, 900 to the nearest 100 and 1000 to the nearest 1000.

b 2363 is 2360 to the nearest 10, 2400 to the nearest 100, and 2000 to the nearest 1000.

c 3799 is 3800 to the nearest 10, 3800 to the nearest 100, and 4000 to the nearest 1000.

d 281 is 280 to the nearest 10, 300 to the nearest 100, and 0 to the nearest 1000.

Example 9.2 ▷

Round off each of these numbers to: **i** the nearest whole number **ii** one decimal place **iii** two decimal places.

a 9.359   **b** 4.323   **c** 5.999

a 9.359 is 9 to the nearest whole number, 9.4 to 1 dp, and 9.36 to 2 dp.

b 4.323 is 4 to the nearest whole number, 4.3 to 1 dp, and 4.32 to 2 dp.

c 5.999 is 6 to the nearest whole number, 6.0 to 1 dp, and 6.00 to 2 dp.

Exercise 9A

1 Round off each of these numbers to: **i** the nearest 10 **ii** the nearest 100 **iii** the nearest 1000.

   a 3731   **b** 807   **c** 2111   **d** 4086   **e** 265   **f** 3457

   g 4050   **h** 2999   **i** 1039   **j** 192   **k** 3192   **l** 964

2   **i**   What is the mass being weighed by each scale to the nearest 100 g?

     ii   Estimate the mass being weighed to the nearest 10 g.

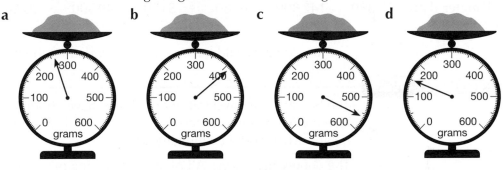

3   **i**   What is the volume of the liquid in each measuring cylinder to the nearest 10 ml?

     ii   Estimate the volume of liquid to the nearest whole number.

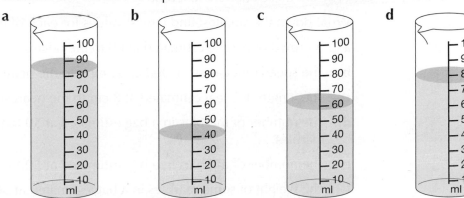

4 Round off each of these numbers to: **i** the nearest whole number **ii** one decimal place **iii** two decimal places.

   a 4.721   **b** 3.073   **c** 2.634   **d** 1.932   **e** 0.785   **f** 0.927

   g 3.925   **h** 2.648   **i** 3.182   **j** 3.475   **k** 1.459   **l** 1.863

5 How long are each of these ropes to: **i** the nearest 100 cm **ii** the nearest 10 cm
iii the nearest cm **iv** the nearest mm?

a

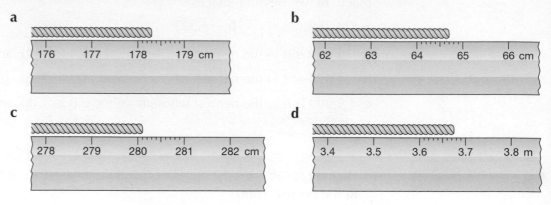

176   177   178   179 cm

b

62   63   64   65   66 cm

c

278   279   280   281   282 cm

d

3.4   3.5   3.6   3.7   3.8 m

6 **a** The following are the diameters of the planets in kilometres. Round off each one
to the nearest 1000 km. Then place the planets in order of size, starting with the
smallest.

Planet	Earth	Jupiter	Mars	Mercury	Neptune	Pluto	Saturn	Uranus	Venus
Diameter (km)	12 800	142 800	6780	5120	49 500	2284	120 660	51 100	12 100

b What would happen if you rounded off the diameters to the nearest 10 000 km?

Extension Work

The headteacher says: 'All of our classes have about 30 pupils in them.'
Given this number is to the nearest 10, what is the smallest class there could
be and what would be the largest?

The deputy head says: 'All of the cars driving past the school are doing about
30 mph.' Given this number is to the nearest 10, what is the lowest speed the
cars could be doing and what would be the highest?

Why are these answers different?

Write down the smallest and largest values for each of the following.

a A crowd of people estimated at 80 to the nearest 10 people.

b The speed of a car estimated at 80 mph to the nearest 10 mph.

c The length of a leaf estimated at 8 cm to the nearest centimetre.

d The number of marbles in a bag estimated at 50 to the nearest 10
marbles.

e The number of marbles in a bag estimated at 50 to the nearest marble.

f The weight of some marbles in a bag estimated at 500 grams to the
nearest 10 grams.

The four operations

Mr Jensen takes his family on a car ferry. The charge for the car is £40. On top of this he pays the standard adult fare for himself. Children are charged half the adult fare and pets are charged £5. The total cost for their crossing is £85. How much is the standard adult fare?

Example 9.3 ▶

a Find the product of 9 and 56.   b Find the remainder when 345 is divided by 51.

a Product means 'multiply'. So, $9 \times 56 = 9 \times 50 + 9 \times 6 = 450 + 54 = 504$.

b $345 \div 51 \approx 350 \div 50 = 7$. So, $7 \times 51 = 350 + 7 = 357$ which is too big.
$6 \times 51 = 306$, which gives $345 - 306 = 39$. The remainder is 39.

Example 9.4 ▶

A box of biscuits costs £1.99. How much will 28 boxes cost?

The easiest way to do this is: $28 \times £2$ minus 28p $= £56 - 28p = £55.72$.

Example 9.5 ▶

Mr Smith travels from Edinburgh (E) to Liverpool (L) and then to Bristol (B). Mr Jones travels directly from Edinburgh to Bristol. Use the distance chart to find out how much further Mr Smith travels than Mr Jones.

Mr Smith travels $226 + 237 = 463$ miles. Mr Jones travels 383 miles.
$463 - 383 = 80$
So, Mr Smith travels 80 miles further.

	E	L	B
E		226	383
L	226		237
B	383	237	

Exercise 9B

1 How long does a train journey take if the train leaves at 10.32 am and arrives at 1.12 pm?

2 Which mark is better: seventeen out of twenty or forty out of fifty?

3 How much does it cost to fill a 51-litre petrol tank at 99p per litre?

4 a A company has 197 boxes to move by van. The van can carry 23 boxes at a time. How many trips must the van make to move all the boxes?

b The same van does 34 miles to the gallon of petrol. Each trip above is 31 miles. Can the van deliver all the boxes if it has 8 gallons of petrol in the tank?

5 Find the sum and product of: a 5, 7 and 20   b 2, 38 and 50

6 Rajid has between 50 and 60 books. He arranged them in piles of four and found that he had one pile of three left over. He then arranged them in piles of five and found that he had one pile of four left over. How many books does Rajid have?

7 The local video shop is having a sale. Videos are £4.99 each or five for £20.

   a What is the cost of three videos?

   b What is the cost of ten videos?

   c What is the greatest number of video you can buy with £37?

8 **a** Three consecutive integers have a sum of 90. What are they?

   b Two consecutive integers have a product of 132. What are they?

   c Explain why there is more than one answer to this problem:

      Two consecutive integers have a difference of 1. What are they?

Extension Work

The magic number of this magic square is 50.

That means that the numbers in every row, in every column and in both diagonals add up to 50.

However, there are many more ways to make 50 by adding four numbers. For example, each of the following sets of 4 numbers from the magic square makes 50.

5	18	11	16
12	15	6	17
14	9	20	7
19	8	13	10

5	18
12	15

5	16
19	10

18	11
8	13

How many more arrangements of four numbers can you find that add up to 50?

BODMAS

The following are instructions for making a cup of tea.

Can you put them in the right order?

Drink tea   Empty teapot   Fill kettle   Put milk in cup   Put teabag in teapot

Switch on kettle   Wait for tea to brew   Rinse teapot with hot water   Pour boiling water in teapot   Pour out tea

It is important that things are done in the right order. In mathematical operations there are rules about this.

The order of operations is called **BODMAS**, which stands for **B** (Brackets), **O** (Order or pOwer), **D M** (Division and Multiplication) and **A S** (Addition and Subtraction).

Operations are always done in this order, which means that brackets are done first, followed by powers, then multiplication and division, and finally addition and subtraction.

Example 9.6 ▶

Circle the operation that you do first in each of these calculations. Then work out each one.

a $2 + 6 \div 2$ **b** $32 - 4 \times 5$ **c** $6 \div 3 - 1$ **d** $6 \div (3 - 1)$

a Division is done before addition, so you get $2 + 6 \div 2 = 2 + 3 = 5$.
b Multiplication is done before subtraction, so you get $32 - 4 \times 5 = 32 - 20 = 12$.
c Division is done before subtraction, so you get $6 \div 3 - 1 = 2 - 1 = 1$.
d Brackets are done first, so you get $6 \div (3 - 1) = 6 \div 2 = 3$.

Example 9.7 ▶

Work out each of the following, showing each step of the calculation.

a $1 + 3^2 \times 4 - 2$ **b** $(1 + 3)^2 \times (4 - 2)$

a The order will be power, multiplication, addition, subtraction (the last two can be interchanged). This gives:
$$1 + 3^2 \times 4 - 2 = 1 + 9 \times 4 - 2 = 1 + 36 - 2 = 37 - 2 = 35$$
b The order will be brackets (both of them), power, multiplication. This gives:
$$(1 + 3)^2 \times (4 - 2) = 4^2 \times 2 = 16 \times 2 = 32$$

Example 9.8 ▶

Add brackets to each of the following to make the calculation true.

a $5 + 1 \times 4 = 24$ **b** $1 + 3^2 - 4 = 12$ **c** $24 \div 6 - 2 = 6$

Decide which operation is done first.

a $(5 + 1) \times 4 = 24$
b $(1 + 3)^2 - 4 = 12$
c $24 \div (6 - 2) = 6$

Exercise 9C

1 Write down the operation that you do first in each of these calculations. Then work out each one.

a $2 + 3 \times 6$ **b** $12 - 6 \div 3$ **c** $5 \times 5 + 2$ **d** $12 \div 4 - 2$
e $(2 + 3) \times 6$ **f** $(12 - 3) \div 3$ **g** $5 \times (5 + 2)$ **h** $12 \div (4 - 2)$

2 Work out the following showing each step of the calculation.

a $2 \times 3 + 4$ **b** $2 \times (3 + 4)$ **c** $2 + 3 \times 4$ **d** $(2 + 3) \times 4$
e $4 \times 4 - 4$ **f** $5 + 3^2 + 6$ **g** $5 \times (3^2 + 6)$ **h** $3^2 - (5 - 2)$
i $(2 + 3) \times (4 + 5)$ **j** $(2^2 + 3) \times (4 + 5)$ **k** $4 \div 4 + 4 \div 4$
l $44 \div 4 + 4$ **m** $(6 + 2)^2$ **n** $6^2 + 2^2$ **o** $3^2 + 4 \times 6$

3 Add brackets to each of the following to make the calculation true.

a $2 \times 5 + 4 = 18$ **b** $2 + 6 \times 3 = 24$ **c** $2 + 3 \times 1 + 6 = 35$
d $5 + 2^2 \times 1 = 9$ **e** $3 + 2^2 = 25$ **f** $3 \times 4 + 3 + 7 = 28$
g $3 + 4 \times 7 + 1 = 35$ **h** $3 + 4 \times 7 + 1 = 50$ **i** $9 - 5 - 2 = 6$
j $9 - 5 \times 2 = 8$ **k** $4 + 4 + 4 \div 2 = 6$ **l** $1 + 4^2 - 9 - 2 = 18$

4 One of the calculations $2 \times 3^2 = 36$ and $2 \times 3^2 = 18$ is wrong. Which is it and how could you add brackets to make it true?

5 Work out the value of each of these.

a $(4 + 4) \div (4 + 4)$ b $(4 \times 4) \div (4 + 4)$ c $(4 + 4 + 4) \div 4$

d $4 \times (4 - 4) + 4$ e $(4 \times 4 + 4) \div 4$ f $(4 + 4 + 4) \div 2$

g $4 + 4 - 4 \div 4$ h $(4 + 4) \times (4 \div 4)$ i $(4 + 4) + 4 \div 4$

Extension   **Work**

In Question 5, each calculation, apart from **f**, was made up of four 4s.

Work out the value of   a $44 \div 4 - 4$ b $4 \times 4 - 4 \div 4$ c $4 \times 4 + 4 - 4$

Can you make other calculations using four 4s to give answers that you have not yet obtained in Question 5 or in the three calculations above?

Do as many as you can and see whether you can make all the values up to 20.

Repeat with five 5s. For example:

$$(5 + 5) \div 5 - 5 \div 5 = 1 \quad (5 \times 5 - 5) \div (5 + 5) = 2$$

Long multiplication and long division

Example 9.9 ▷

Work out 36×43.

Below are four examples of the ways this calculation can be done. The answer is 1548.

Box method (partitioning)	Column method (expanded working)	Column method (compacted working)	Chinese method

Box method (partitioning)

×	30	6	
40	1200	240	1440
3	90	18	108
			1548

Column method (expanded working)

$$
\begin{array}{r}
36 \\
\times\ \ 43 \\
\hline
18 \quad (3 \times 6) \\
90 \quad (3 \times 30) \\
240 \quad (40 \times 6) \\
1200 \quad (40 \times 30) \\
\hline
1548 \\
\end{array}
$$

Column method (compacted working)

$$
\begin{array}{r}
36 \\
\times\ \ 43 \\
\hline
108 \quad (3 \times 36) \\
1440 \quad (40 \times 36) \\
\hline
1548 \\
\end{array}
$$

Chinese method

(lattice multiplication grid for $36 \times 43 = 1548$)

Example 9.10 ▷

Work out $543 \div 31$.

Below are two examples of the ways this can be done. The answer is 17, remainder 16.

Subtracting multiples

$$
\begin{array}{r}
543 \\
-\ 310 \quad (10 \times 31) \\
\hline
233 \\
-\ 155 \quad (5 \times 31) \\
\hline
78 \\
-\ 62 \quad (2 \times 31) \\
\hline
16 \\
\end{array}
$$

Traditional method

$$
\begin{array}{r}
17 \\
31\overline{)543} \\
\underline{31} \\
233 \\
\underline{217} \\
16 \\
\end{array}
$$

1. Work out each of the following long multiplication problems. Use any method you are happy with.

   a 17×23 b 32×42 c 19×45 d 56×46

   e 12×346 f 32×541 g 27×147 h 39×213

2. Work out each of the following long division problems. Use any method you are happy with. Some of the problems will have a remainder.

   a $684 \div 19$ b $966 \div 23$ c $972 \div 36$ d $625 \div 25$

   e $930 \div 38$ f $642 \div 24$ g $950 \div 33$ h $800 \div 42$

Decide whether the following nine problems involve long multiplication or long division. Then do the appropriate calculation, showing your method clearly.

3. Each day 17 Jumbo jets fly from London to San Francisco. Each jet can carry up to 348 passengers. How many people can travel from London to San Francisco each day?

4. A company has 897 boxes to move by van. The van can carry 23 boxes at a time. How many trips must the van make to move all the boxes?

5. The same van does 34 miles to a gallon of petrol. How many miles can it do if the petrol tank holds 18 gallons?

6. The school photocopier can print 82 sheets a minute. If it runs without stopping for 45 minutes, how many sheets will it print?

7. The RE department has printed 525 sheets on Buddhism. These are put into folders in sets of 35. How many folders are there?

8. a To raise money, Wath Running Club are going to do a relay race from Wath to Edinburgh, which is 384 kilometres. Each runner will run 24 kilometres. How many runners will be needed to cover the distance?

   b Sponsorship will bring in £32 per kilometre. How much money will the club raise?

9. Blank CDs are 45p each. How much will a box of 35 disks cost? Give your answer in pounds.

10. The daily newspaper sells advertising by the square inch. On Monday, it sells 232 square inches at £15 per square inch. How much money does it get from this advertising?

11. The local library has 13 000 books. Each shelf holds 52 books. How many shelves are there?

Another way of multiplying two two-digit numbers together is the 'Funny Face' method.

This shows how to do 26×57.

$$26 \times 57 = (20 + 6) \times (50 + 7)$$

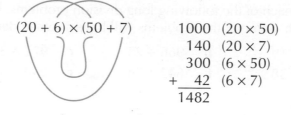

$(20 + 6) \times (50 + 7)$

$$
\begin{array}{ll}
1000 & (20 \times 50) \\
140 & (20 \times 7) \\
300 & (6 \times 50) \\
+\quad 42 & (6 \times 7) \\
\hline
1482 &
\end{array}
$$

Do a poster showing a calculation using the 'Funny Face' method.

Efficient calculations

You should have your own calculator, so that you can get used to it. Make sure that you understand how to use the basic functions ($\times$, $\div$, $+$, $-$) and the square, square root and brackets keys.

Example 9.11 ▷

Use a calculator to work out: **a** $\dfrac{242 + 118}{88 - 72}$ **b** $\dfrac{63 \times 224}{32 \times 36}$

The line that separates the top numbers from the bottom numbers acts both as a divide sign ($\div$) and as brackets.

a Key the calculation as $(242 + 118) \div (88 - 72) = 22.5$.

b Key the calculation as $(63 \times 224) \div (32 \times 36) = 12.25$.

Example 9.12 ▷

Use a calculator to work out: **a** $\sqrt{1764}$ **b** 23.4^2 **c** $52.3 - (30.4 - 17.3)$

a Some calculators need the square root after the number has been keyed, some need it before: $\sqrt{1764} = 42$

b Most calculators have a special key for squaring: $23.4^2 = 547.56$

c This can be keyed in exactly as it reads: $52.3 - (30.4 - 17.3) = 39.2$

Exercise 9E

1 Without using a calculator, work out the value of each of these.

a $\dfrac{17 + 8}{7 - 2}$ **b** $\dfrac{53 - 8}{3.5 - 2}$ **c** $\dfrac{19.2 - 1.7}{5.6 - 3.1}$

2 Use a calculator to do the calculations in Question 1. Do you get the same answers?

For each part, write down the sequence of keys that you pressed to get the answer.

3 Work out the value of each of these. Round off your answers to 1 dp.

a $\dfrac{194 + 866}{122 + 90}$ b $\dfrac{213 + 73}{63 - 19}$ c $\dfrac{132 + 88}{78 - 28}$ d $\dfrac{792 + 88}{54 - 21}$

e $\dfrac{790 \times 84}{24 \times 28}$ f $\dfrac{642 \times 24}{87 - 15}$ g $\dfrac{107 + 853}{24 \times 16}$ h $\dfrac{57 - 23}{18 - 7.8}$

4 Estimate the answer to $\dfrac{231 + 167}{78 - 32}$

Now use a calculator to work out the answer to 1 dp. Is it about the same?

5 Work out the following:

a $\sqrt{42.25}$ b $\sqrt{68.89}$ c 2.6^2 d 3.9^2

e $\sqrt{(23.8 + 66.45)}$ f $\sqrt{(7 - 5.04)}$ g $(5.2 - 1.8)^2$ h $(2.5 + 6.1)^2$

6 Work out the following:

a $8.3 - (4.2 - 1.9)$ b $12.3 + (3.2 - 1.7)^2$ c $(3.2 + 1.9)^2 - (5.2 - 2.1)^2$

7 Use a calculator to find the quotient and the remainder when:

a 985 is divided by 23 b 802 is divided by 36

8 A calculator shows an answer of:

2.33333333333

Write this as a mixed number or a top heavy fraction.

Extension **Work**

Time calculations are difficult to do on a calculator as there are not 100 minutes in an hour. So, you need to know either the decimal equivalents of all the divisions of an hour or the way to work them out. For example: 15 minutes is 0.25 of an hour.

Copy and complete this table for some of the decimal equivalents to fractions of an hour.

Time (min)	5	6	12	15	20	30	40	45	54	55
Fraction	$\frac{1}{12}$	$\frac{1}{10}$		$\frac{1}{4}$	$\frac{1}{3}$				$\frac{9}{10}$	
Decimal	0.083		0.2	0.25			0.667			0.917

When a time is given as a decimal and it is not one of those in the table above, you need a way to work it out in hours and minutes. For example:

3.4578 hours: subtract 3 to give 0.4578, then multiply by 60 to give 27.468

This is 27 minutes to the nearest minute. So, 3.4578 ≈ 3 hours 27 minutes.

1 Find each of the following decimal times as a time in hours and minutes.

a 2.5 h b 3.25 h c 4.75 h d 3.1 h

e 4.6 h f 3.3333 h g 1.15 h h 4.3 h

i 0.45 h j 0.95 h k 3.666 h

2 Find each of the following times in hours and minutes as a decimal time.

a 2 h 40 min b 1 h 45 min c 2 h 18 min d 1 h 20 min

Calculating with measurements

The following table shows the relationship between the common metric units.

1000	100	10	1	0.1	0.01	0.001
km			m		cm	mm
kg			g			mg
			l		cl	ml

Example 9.13 ▷

Add together 1.23 m, 46 cm and 0.034 km.

First convert all the lengths to the same unit.

1000	100	10	1	0.1	0.01	0.001
km			m		cm	mm
			1	2	3	
				4	6	
0	0	3	4			

The answer is 0.035 69 km or 35.69 m or 3569 cm. 35.69 m is the sensible answer.

Example 9.14 ▷

A recipe needs 550 grams of flour to make a cake. How many 1 kg bags of flour will be needed to make six cakes?

Six cakes will need $6 \times 550 = 3300$ g, which will need four bags of flour.

Example 9.15 ▷

What unit would you use to measure each of these?

a   Width of a football field

b   Length of a pencil

c   Weight of a car

d   Spoonful of medicine

Choose a sensible unit. Sometimes there is more than one answer.

a   Metre   b   Centimetre   c   Kilogram   d   Millilitre

Example 9.16 ▷

Convert: a   6 cm to mm   b   1250 g to kg   c   5 l to cl

You need to know the conversion factors.

a   1 cm = 10 mm: $6 \times 10 = 60$ mm

b   1000 g = 1 kg: $1250 \div 1000 = 1.25$ kg

c   1 l = 100 cl: 5 l = $5 \times 100 = 500$ cl

Exercise 9F

1 Convert each of the following lengths to centimetres.

   a 60 mm   **b** 2 m   **c** 743 mm
   d 0.007 km   **e** 12.35 m

2 Convert each of the following lengths to kilometres.

   a 456 m   **b** 7645 m   **c** 6532 cm
   d 21 358 mm   **e** 54 m

3 Convert each of the following lengths to millimetres.

   a 34 cm   **b** 3 m   **c** 3 km
   d 35.6 cm   **e** 0.7 cm

4 Convert each of the following masses to kilograms.

   a 3459 g   **b** 215 g   **c** 65 120 g
   d 21 g   **e** 210 g

5 Convert each of the following masses to grams.

   a 4 kg   **b** 4.32 kg   **c** 0.56 kg
   d 0.007 kg   **e** 6.784 kg

6 Convert each of the following capacities to litres.

   a 237 cl   **b** 3097 ml   **c** 1862 cl
   d 48 cl   **e** 96 427 ml

7 Convert each of the following times to hours and minutes.

   a 70 min   **b** 125 min   **c** 87 min
   d 200 min   **e** 90 min

8 Add together each of the following groups of measurements and give the answer in an appropriate unit.

   a 1.78 m, 39 cm, 0.006 km
   b 0.234 kg, 60 g, 0.004 kg
   c 2.3 l, 46 cl, 726 ml
   d 0.0006 km, 23 mm, 3.5 cm

9 Fill in each missing unit.

   a A two-storey house is about 7…… high.
   b John weighs about 47……
   c Mary lives about 2…… from school.
   d Ravid ran a marathon in 3……

10 Read the value from each of the following scales.

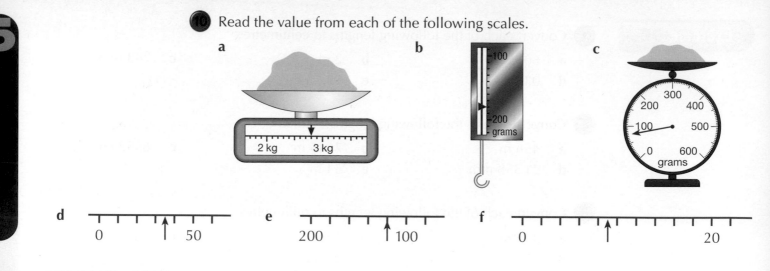

a

b

c

d
0   50

e
200   100

f
0   20

Area is measured in square millimetres (mm^2), square centimetres (cm^2), square metres (m^2) and square kilometres (km^2).

This square shows 1 square centimetre reproduced exactly.

You can fit 100 square millimetres inside this square because a 1 centimetre square is 10 mm by 10 mm.

10 mm

10 mm

How many square centimetres are there in 1 square metre?

How many square metres are there in 1 square kilometre?

1   What unit would you use to measure the area of each of these?
    a   Football field
    b   Photograph
    c   Fingernail
    d   National park
    e   Pacific Ocean
    f   Stamp

2   Convert:
    a   24 cm^2 to mm^2
    b   6 km^2 to m^2
    c   4000 mm^2 to cm^2
    d   3 456 000 m^2 to km^2

3   Look up the areas of some countries on the Internet or in an encyclopaedia.
    a   Which are the three biggest countries (in terms of area) in the world?
    b   Which is the biggest country (in terms of area) in Europe?

Solving problems

MATHEMATICAL MICE

Mrs Farmer is frightened of mice. One day, she finds three mice in her kitchen. A large one, a medium-sized one and a small one.

She tries to scare them out but they are Mathematical Mice who will only leave when a dice is rolled.

When the dice shows 1 or 2, the small mouse goes through the door.

When the dice shows 3 or 4, the medium-sized mouse goes through the door.

When the dice shows 5 or 6, the big mouse goes through the door.

For example: Mrs Farmer rolls the dice. She gets 3, so the medium-sized mouse goes through the door. Next, she rolls 5, so the big mouse goes through the door. Next, she rolls 4, so the medium-sized mouse comes back through the door. Then she rolls 2, so the small mouse leaves. Finally, she rolls 4, so the medium-sized mouse leaves and all three are out of the kitchen.

Can you find a rule for the number of throws that it takes to get out all the mice?

What if there were two mice, or six mice?

Before you start, you should think about how you are going to record your results.

You should make sure that you explain in writing what you are going to do.

If you come up with an idea, you should write it down and explain it or test it.

LEVEL BOOSTER

5
I can write down and simplify ratios.
I can calculate a percentage of a quantity.
I can convert one metric unit to another.

6
I can convert compound metric units.
I can solve more complex problems independently.

5

1 *2005 Paper 1*

A meal in a restaurant costs the same for each person.

For **11** people the total cost is **£253**.

What is the total cost for 12 people?

2 *2004 Paper 1*

Steve needs to put **1 litre** of water in a bucket.
He has a **500 ml** jug.

Explain how he can measure 1 litre of water.

3 *2005 4–6 Paper 1*

a I weigh a melon.

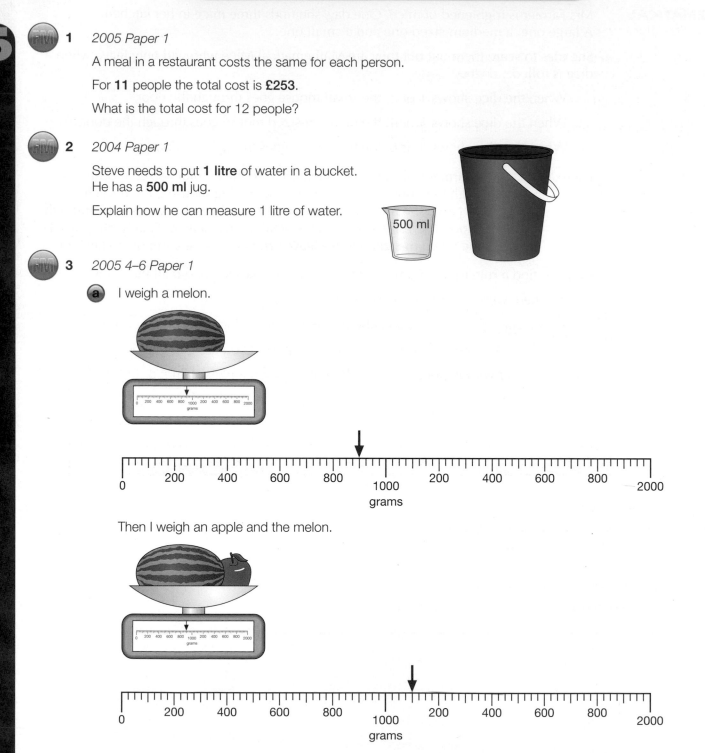

Then I weigh an apple and the melon.

Complete the sentences below, writing in the missing numbers:

The **melon** weighs ... grams.

The **apple** weighs ... grams.

b How many **grams** are in one **kilogram**?

Which one of the following numbers is correct?

1   10   100   1000   10 000

4 *2000 Paper 2*

a A club wants to take 3000 people on a journey to London using coaches. Each coach can carry people. How many coaches do they need?

b Each coach costs £420. What is the total cost of the coaches?

c How much is each person's share of the cost?

5 *2001 Paper 2*

The label on a pot of yoghurt shows this information.

How many grams of protein does 100 g of yoghurt provide?

YOGHURT 125 g	
Each 125 g provides	
Energy	430 kJ
Protein	4.5 g
Carbohydrate	11.1 g
Fat	4.5 g

6 *2004 Paper 1*

Copy the table and write down the missing numbers.

The first row is done for you.

First number	Second number	Sum of first and second numbers	Product of first and second numbers
3	6	9	18
5	−3		
−8		−5	

energy. Scientists
rbon footprint
uch energy

Fascinating facts

Our homes use 30% of the total energy used in the UK.

- The average yearly carbon dioxide emissions in the UK are 9.4 tonnes per person.

- A rule for working out the average yearly carbon dioxide emissions of people in the USA is to multiply the UK figure by 3 and subtract 8.4. This gives $9.4 \times 3 - 8.4 = 19.8$ tonnes per person.

- If we turn down the thermostat by one degree we would save 300 kg of carbon dioxide per household per year.

- A family car with a petrol engine uses about 160 grams per kilometre, compared with about 100 grams per kilometre for a small car or 300 grams per kilometre for a large 4 × 4.

Carbon calculator

1 If you take the bus to school you can work out the emissions from a bus.
Carbon dioxide emission (kg) = Distance (km) × 0.17

a Work out the carbon dioxide emission for a distance of 13 kilometres. Give your answer in grams.

b A school bus holds 87 passengers. Work out the carbon dioxide emissions per person.

c Work out the carbon dioxide emissions for a person travelling 13 kilometres by family car.

Food miles

2 The food you eat may have travelled across the globe to reach your plate.

For example:

Strawberries from Turkey: 1760 miles

Peas from Egypt: 2181 miles

Tomatoes from Mexico: 5551 miles

○ How many miles is this altogether?

Round your answer to the nearest 50 miles.

Carbon dioxide emissions per person

3 **a** Work out the difference between the average yearly carbon dioxide emissions of people in the UK and the USA.

b How many people on average would be needed to use one extra tonne of carbon dioxide in the USA compared with the UK?

c A rule for working out the average yearly carbon dioxide emissions of people in China is to add 0.2 to the UK figure and divide by 3. Use this rule to work out the figure for China.

Save energy

4 If 7500 households turn down their thermostat by one degree for a year, how much carbon dioxide would be saved?

Give your answer in tonnes.

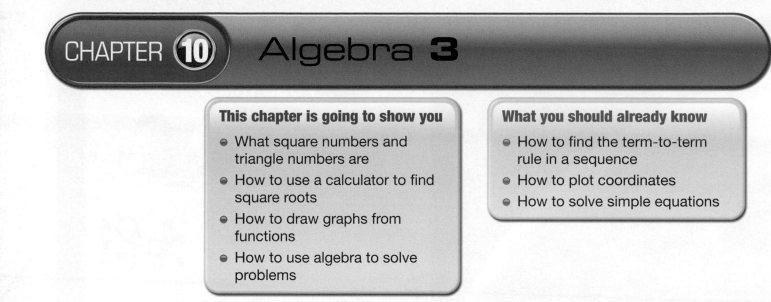

CHAPTER 10 — Algebra 3

This chapter is going to show you
- What square numbers and triangle numbers are
- How to use a calculator to find square roots
- How to draw graphs from functions
- How to use algebra to solve problems

What you should already know
- How to find the term-to-term rule in a sequence
- How to plot coordinates
- How to solve simple equations

Square numbers and square roots

When we multiply any number by itself, the answer is called the **square of the number** or the **number squared**. We call this operation **squaring**. We show it by putting a small 2 at the top right-hand corner of the number being squared. For example:

$$4 \times 4 = 4^2 = 16$$

The result of squaring a number is also called a **square number**. The first ten square numbers are shown below.

1×1	2×2	3×3	4×4	5×5	6×6	7×7	8×8	9×9	10×10
1^2	2^2	3^2	4^2	5^2	6^2	7^2	8^2	9^2	10^2
1	4	9	16	25	36	49	64	81	100

You need to learn all of these.

The **square root** of a number is that number which, when squared, gives the starting number. It is the opposite of finding the square of a number. There are always *two* square roots of a positive number: a positive value and its negative.

A square root is represented by the symbol $\sqrt{}$. For example:

$$\sqrt{1} = 1 \text{ and } -1 \quad \sqrt{4} = 2 \text{ and } -2 \quad \sqrt{9} = 3 \text{ and } -3 \quad \sqrt{16} = 4 \text{ and } -4 \quad \sqrt{25} = 5 \text{ and } -5$$

Only the square root of a square number will give an integer (whole number) as the answer.

Exercise 10A

1 Look at the pattern on the right.
   a Copy this pattern and draw the next two shapes in the pattern.
   b What is special about the total number of dots in each pattern number?
   c What is special about the number of blue dots in each pattern number?
   d What is special about the number of red dots in each pattern number?
   e Write down a connection between square numbers and odd numbers.

Pattern 1   Pattern 2   Pattern 3

1   1 + 3   4 + 5
        4   9

2 $45 = 9 + 36 = 3^2 + 6^2$

Give each of the following numbers as the sum of two square numbers, as above.

a	29	**b**	34	**c**	65	**d**	100	**e**	82
f	25	**g**	85	**h**	73	**i**	106	**j**	58

3 You should have noticed from Question **2f** above that $3^2 + 4^2 = 5^2$.

This is a *special square sum* (made up of only square numbers). There are many to be found. See which of the following pairs of squares will give you a special square sum.

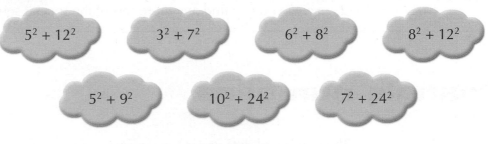

$5^2 + 12^2$ $3^2 + 7^2$ $6^2 + 8^2$ $8^2 + 12^2$

$5^2 + 9^2$ $10^2 + 24^2$ $7^2 + 24^2$

4 Write down the value represented by each of the following. Do not forget to write down the negative value. Do not use a calculator.

a	$\sqrt{16}$	**b**	$\sqrt{36}$	**c**	$\sqrt{4}$	**d**	$\sqrt{49}$	**e**	$\sqrt{1}$
f	$\sqrt{9}$	**g**	$\sqrt{100}$	**h**	$\sqrt{81}$	**i**	$\sqrt{25}$	**j**	$\sqrt{64}$

5 With the aid of a calculator, write down the value represented by each of the following.

a	$\sqrt{289}$	**b**	$\sqrt{961}$	**c**	$\sqrt{529}$	**d**	$\sqrt{2500}$	**e**	$\sqrt{1296}$
f	$\sqrt{729}$	**g**	$\sqrt{3249}$	**h**	$\sqrt{361}$	**i**	$\sqrt{3969}$	**j**	$\sqrt{1764}$

6 Make an estimate of each of the following square roots. Then use your calculator to see how many you got right.

a	$\sqrt{256}$	**b**	$\sqrt{1089}$	**c**	$\sqrt{625}$	**d**	$\sqrt{2704}$	**e**	$\sqrt{1444}$
f	$\sqrt{841}$	**g**	$\sqrt{3481}$	**h**	$\sqrt{441}$	**i**	$\sqrt{4096}$	**j**	$\sqrt{2025}$

7 The solutions to $x^2 = 9$ are $x = 3$ and $x = -3$. These can be written as $x = \pm 3$, which means $x = 3$ and $x = -3$.

Write down the full solution to each of these equations.

a	$x^2 = 16$	**b**	$x^2 = 36$	**c**	$x^2 = 100$	**d**	$x^2 = 1$
e	$x^2 + 1 = 10$	**f**	$x^2 - 3 = 46$	**g**	$x^2 + 7 = 11$		

8 Write down the full solution to each of these equations.

a	$2x^2 = 18$	**b**	$4x^2 = 100$	**c**	$3x^2 = 12$	**d**	$5x^2 = 45$
e	$3x^2 + 5 = 80$	**f**	$4x^2 - 7 = 29$	**g**	$2x^2 + 17 = 115$		

1   **a**   Choose any two square numbers: for example, *m* and *n*.

b   Multiply them together: $m \times n = R$.

c   What is the square root of this result, $\sqrt{R}$?

d   Can you find a connection between this square root and the two starting numbers?

e   Try this again for more square numbers.

f   Is the connection the same no matter what two square numbers you choose?

2   See if you can find any more sets of the special square sums.

Triangle numbers

The number of dots used to make each triangle in this pattern form the sequence of **triangle numbers**.

The first few triangle numbers are   1   3   6

1, 3, 6, 10, 15, 21, 28, 36, 45, ...

You need to remember how to generate the sequence of triangle numbers.

1   Look at the following sequence.

Pattern number	1	2	3	4	5	6	7
Number of blue dots	1	3	6				
Number of yellow dots	0	1	3				
Total number of dots	1	4	9				

a   Continue the sequence for the next three shapes.

b   Complete the table to show the number of dots in each shape.

c   What is special about the number of **blue** dots?

d   What is special about the number of **yellow** dots?

e   What is special about the **total number** of dots in each pattern number?

f   Write down a connection between triangle numbers and square numbers.

2   Look at the numbers in the box on the right.

Write down the numbers that are:

a   square numbers.   **d**   multiples of 5.

b   triangle numbers.   **e**   factors of 100.

c   even numbers.   **f**   prime numbers.

1	2	3	5	6	9
10	13	15	18	21	
25	26	28	29	36	
38	64	75	93	100	

Each of the following numbers can be given as the sum of two triangle numbers. Write each sum in full.

a	7	**b**	24	**c**	16	**d**	31
e	21	**f**	25	**g**	36	**h**	42

4 **a** Write down the first 12 triangle numbers.

b How many of these numbers are: **i** even **ii** odd.

c How many of these numbers are multiples of 3?

d Look at the numbers that are not multiples of 3. What is special about them all?

e Test parts **b** to **d** with the next 12 triangle numbers.

f What do you notice about your answers to part **e**?

Extension **Work**

1 and 36 are both square numbers and triangle numbers. Which are the next two numbers to be both square and triangular? You will need to use a spreadsheet as the numbers are quite large.

Hint: The first is between the 30th and 40th square number and the next is a few below the 300th triangle number.

From mappings to graphs

Think about the function $x \to x + 1$. This represents the relationship 'Add on one'.

The equation $y = x + 1$ is another way of representing this function, and it is easier to use.

Putting these values together to form ordered pairs, we get:

$$(1, 2), (2, 3), (3, 4), (4, 5), (5, 6)$$

We have chosen just five starting points, but we could have chosen many more.

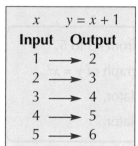

x	$y = x + 1$
Input	**Output**
1	→ 2
2	→ 3
3	→ 4
4	→ 5
5	→ 6

We can use these ordered pairs as coordinates, and plot them on a pair of axes, as shown on the right.

We can join all the points with a straight line. Choose any point on the straight line. Use the first number of the pair of coordinates as the input to the function. You should find that the output is the second number of the coordinate pair.

Notice how we can extend the line into the negative axes. Check that the coordinates still satisfy the function.

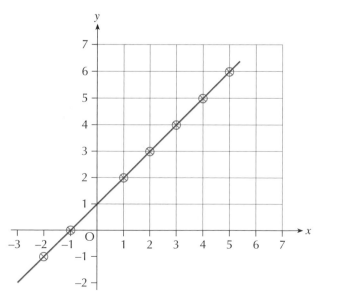

This chapter is going to show you

● How to measure and draw angles
● How to construct triangles and other shapes
● How to construct the perpendicular bisector of a straight line
● How to construct the bisector of an angle
● The geometrical properties of triangles and quadrilaterals

What you should already know

● How to use a protractor to measure and draw angles
● How to calculate angles on a straight line and around a point
● How to calculate angles in a triangle

Measuring and drawing angles

Notice that on a semicircular protractor there are two scales. The outer scale goes from 0° to 180°, and the inner one goes from 180° to 0°. It is important that you use the correct scale.

When measuring or drawing an angle, always decide first whether it is an acute angle or an obtuse angle.

Example 11.1 ▷ First, decide whether the angle to be measured is acute or obtuse. This is an acute angle (less than 90°).

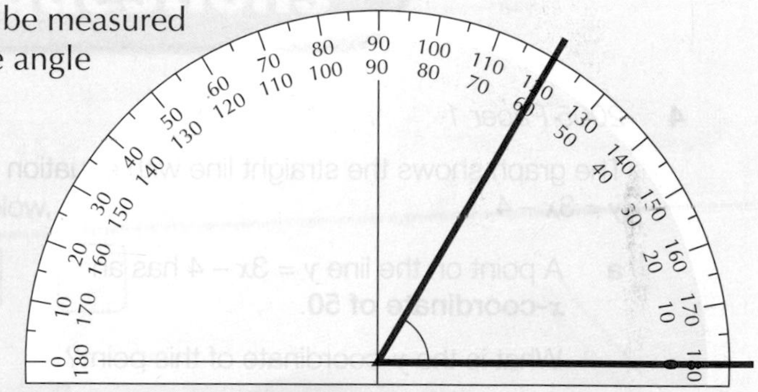

Place the centre of the protractor at the corner of the angle, as in the diagram.

The two angles shown on the protractor scales are 60° and 120°. Since you are measuring an acute angle, the angle is 60° (to the nearest degree).

Example 11.2 ▷ Measure the size of this reflex angle.

First, measure the inside or interior angle. This is an obtuse angle.

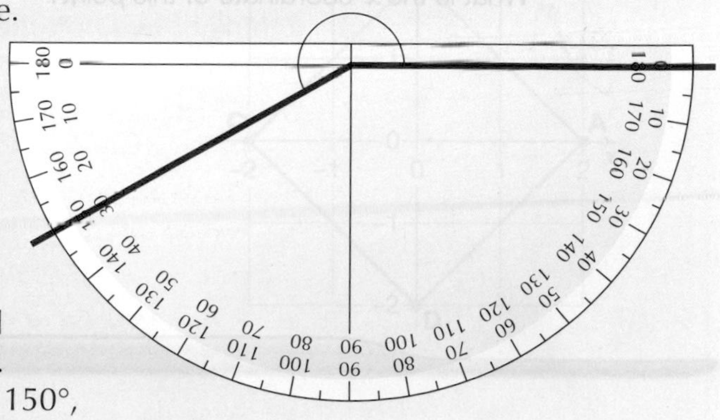

The two angles shown on the protractor scales are 30° and 150°. Since you are measuring an obtuse angle, the angle is 150°.

The size of the reflex angle is found by subtracting this angle from 360°. The reflex angle is therefore 360° − 150°, which is 210° (to the nearest degree).

Exercise 11A

1 Measure the size of each of the following angles, giving your answer to the nearest degree.

a

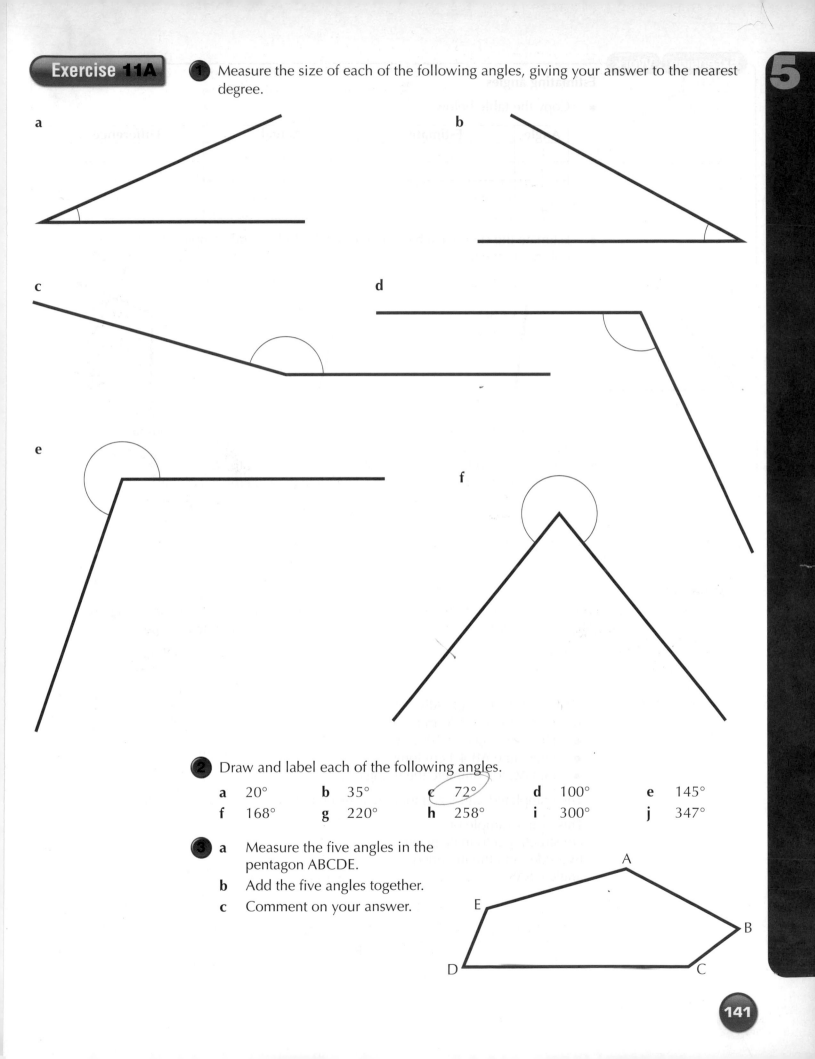

b

c

d

e

f

2 Draw and label each of the following angles.

a 20°	**b** 35°	**c** 72°	**d** 100°	**e** 145°
f 168°	**g** 220°	**h** 258°	**i** 300°	**j** 347°

3 a Measure the five angles in the pentagon ABCDE.

b Add the five angles together.

c Comment on your answer.

Example 11.6 ▷ To construct the mid-point and the perpendicular bisector of a line segment.
  ● Draw a line segment AB of any length.
  ● Set the compasses to any radius which is greater than half the length of AB.
  ● Draw two arcs with their centre at A, above and below AB.
  ● With the compasses set at the same radius, draw two arcs with their centre at B, to intersect the first two arcs at C and D.
  ● Join C and D to intersect AB at X.
  ● X is the mid-point of the line AB.
  ● The line CD is the perpendicular bisector of the line AB.

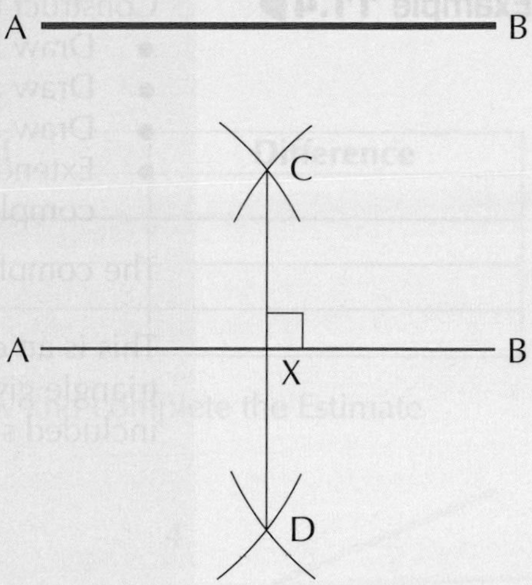

All construction lines should be left on the diagram.

Example 11.7 ▷ To construct the bisector of ∠ABC.
  ● Draw an angle ABC of any size.
  ● Set the compasses to any radius and, with centre at B, draw an arc to intersect BC at X and AB at Y.
  ● With the compasses set to any radius, draw two arcs with centres at X and Y, to intersect at Z.
  ● Join BZ.
  ● BZ is the bisector of ∠ABC.
  ● ∠ABZ = ∠CBZ.

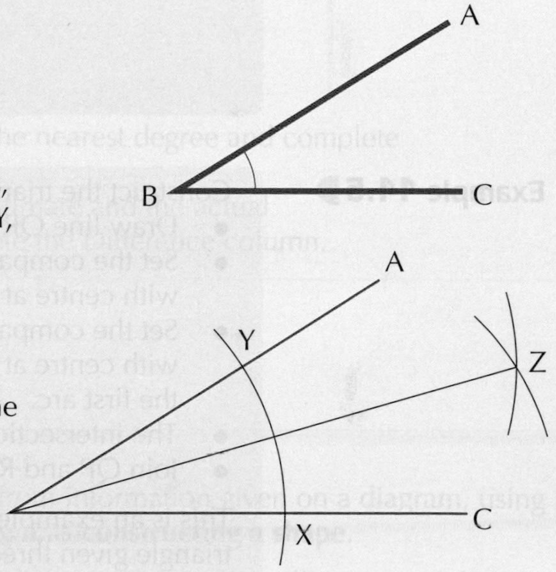

All construction lines should be left on the diagram.

Exercise 11B

① Construct each of the following triangles. Remember to label all lines and angles.

a

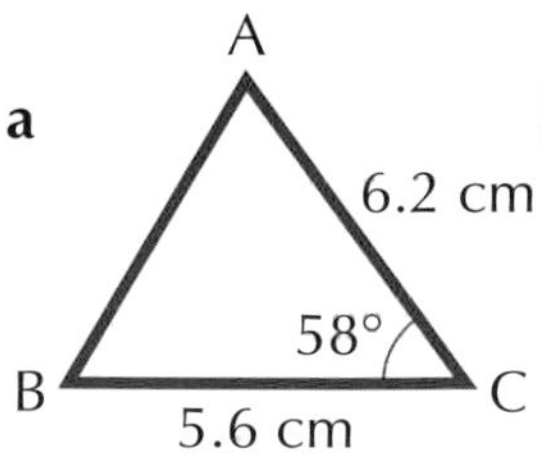

A
6.2 cm
58°
B 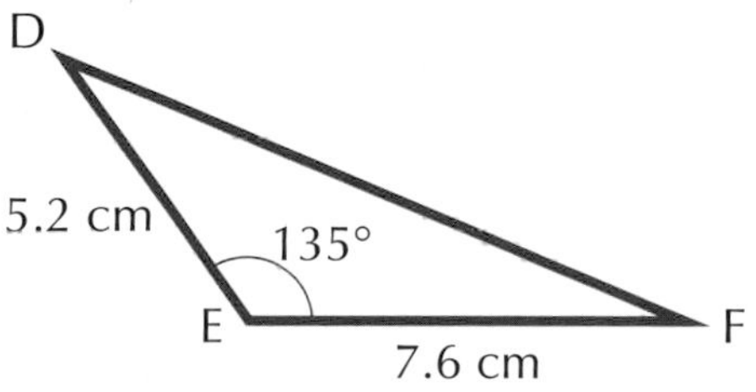
5.6 cm
C

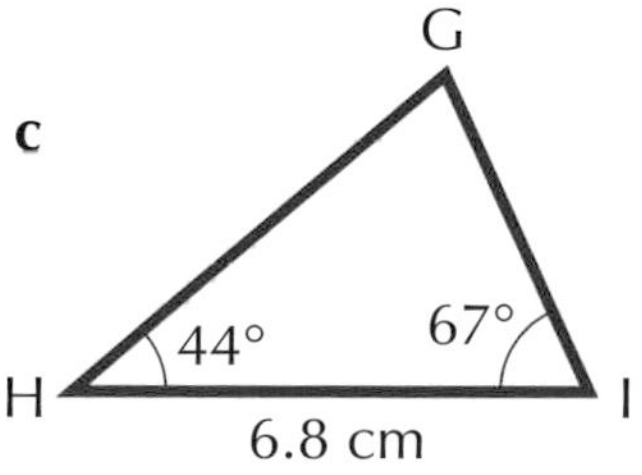

b

D
5.2 cm
135°
E
7.6 cm
F

c

G
44°   67°
H
6.8 cm
I

d

J
6.4 cm
5.7 cm
K
8.6 cm
L

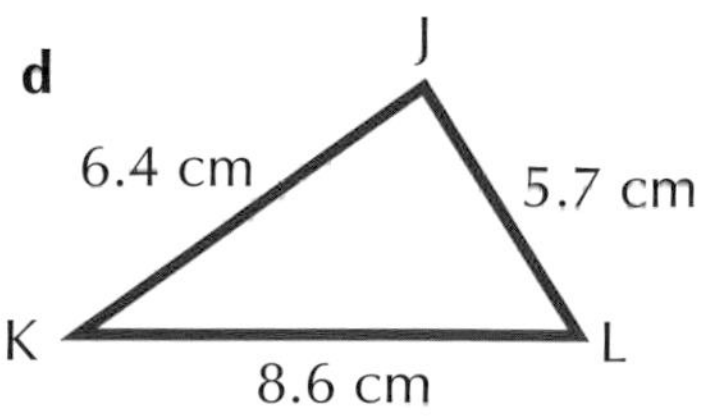

② a Construct the triangle PQR.
  b Measure the size of ∠P and ∠R to the nearest degree.
  c Measure the length of the line PR to the nearest millimetre.

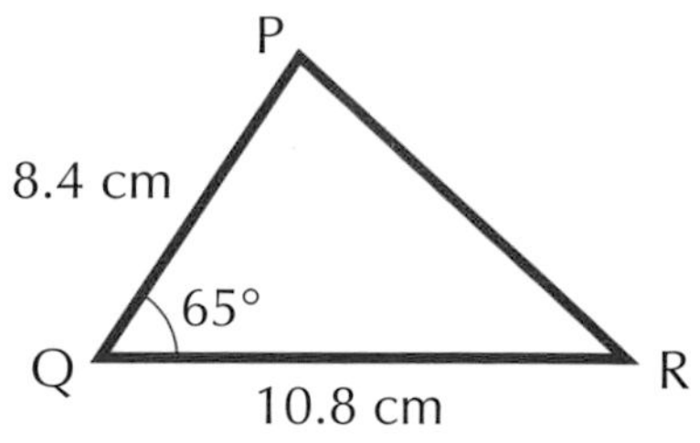

P
8.4 cm
65°
Q
10.8 cm
R

3　**a**　Construct the triangle ABC with ∠A = 100°, ∠B = 36° and AB = 8.4 cm.

　　b　Construct the triangle XYZ with XY = 6.5 cm, XZ = 4.3 cm and YZ = 5.8 cm.

4　**a**　Construct the trapezium ABCD.

　　b　Measure the size of ∠B to the nearest degree.

　　c　Measure the length of the lines AB and BC to the nearest millimetre.

5　**a**　Draw a line AB 6 cm long. Construct the perpendicular bisector of AB.

　　b　Draw a line CD 8.5 cm long. Construct the perpendicular bisector of CD.

6　**a**　Draw an angle of 48°. Construct the bisector of the angle.

　　b　Draw an angle of 90°. Construct the bisector of the angle.

　　c　Draw an angle of 120°. Construct the bisector of the angle.

Extension **Work**

1　Construct the parallelogram ABCD with AB = 7.4 cm, AD = 6.4 cm, ∠A = 50° and ∠B = 130°.

2　**a**　Construct the quadrilateral PQRS.

　　b　Measure ∠P and ∠Q to the nearest degree.

　　c　Measure the length of the line PQ to the nearest millimetre.

3　If you have access to ICT facilities, find out how to draw triangles using computer software packages such as LOGO.

Solving geometrical problems

Types of triangle

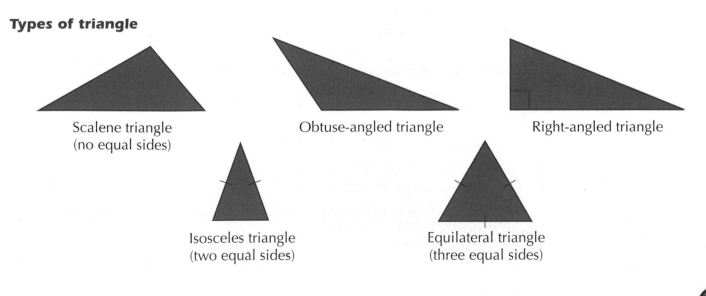

Scalene triangle
(no equal sides)

Obtuse-angled triangle

Right-angled triangle

Isosceles triangle
(two equal sides)

Equilateral triangle
(three equal sides)

Types of quadrilateral

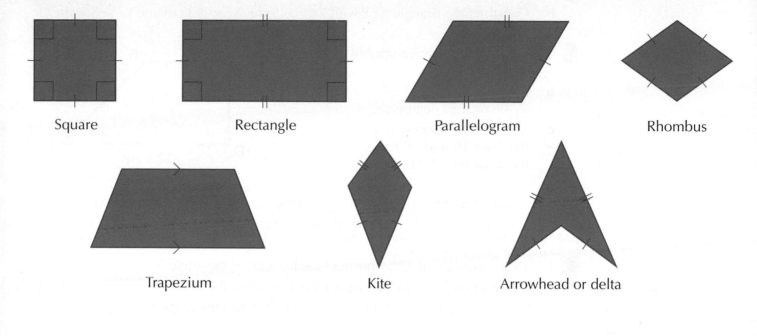

Square   Rectangle   Parallelogram   Rhombus

Trapezium   Kite   Arrowhead or delta

Exercise 11C

1 Which quadrilaterals have the following properties?
  a Four equal sides
  b Two different pairs of equal sides
  c Two pairs of parallel sides
  d Only one pair of parallel sides
  e Adjacent sides equal
  f Diagonals are equal in length
  g Diagonals bisect each other
  h Diagonals are perpendicular to each other
  i Diagonals intersect at right angles outside the shape

2 Explain the difference between:
  a a square and a rectangle.
  b a rhombus and a parallelogram.
  c a kite and an arrowhead.

3 How many different triangles can be constructed on this 3 by 3 pin-board?

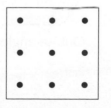

Use square dotted paper to record your triangles. Below each one, write down what type of triangle it is.

Copy this square on a piece of card. Then draw in the two diagonals and cut out the four triangles.

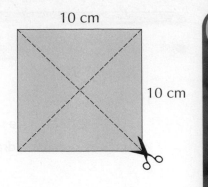

How many different triangles or quadrilaterals can you make with the following?

a Four of the triangles

b Three of the triangles

c Two of the triangles

Extension Work

How many distinct quadrilaterals can be constructed on this 3 by 3 pin-board?

Use square dotted paper to record your quadrilaterals. Below each one, write down what type of quadrilateral it is.

LEVEL BOOSTER

5 I can draw and measure angles.

I can understand the simple geometrical properties of triangles and quadrilaterals.

6 I can construct triangles from given data.

I can construct the mid-point and the perpendicular bisector of a straight line.

I can construct the bisector of an angle.

I can solve problems using the geometrical properties of triangles and quadrilaterals.

5

1 *2002 Paper 2*

Here is a sketch of a sector of a circle.

Make an **accurate drawing** of the sector.

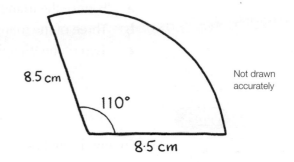

8.5 cm

110°

8·5 cm

Not drawn accurately

2 *2006 Paper 2*

Some statements in the table are true. Some are false.

Copy the table and, beside each statement, write **true** or **false**.

For true statements you must **draw an example.**

The first one is done for you.

Statement	Write **true** or **false**. If true, draw an example.
Some triangles have one right angle and two acute angles.	true 
Some triangles have three right angles.	
Some triangles have three acute angles.	
Some triangles have one obtuse angle and two acute angles.	
Some triangles have two obtuse angles and one acute angle.	

3 *2000 Paper 1*

Look at these angles.

 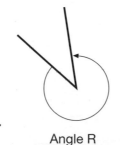 

Angle P   Angle Q   Angle R   Angle S   Angle T

a One of the angles measures **120°**

Write its letter.

b Complete the drawing below to show an angle of **157°**

Label the angle 157°

4   *2003 Paper 1*

Use compasses to construct a triangle that has sides **8 cm**, **6 cm** and **7 cm**.

Leave in your construction lines.

One side of the triangle is drawn for you to copy.

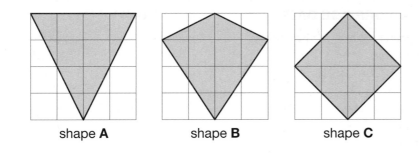

8 cm

5   *2004 Paper 1*

The shapes below are drawn on square grids.

shape **A**   shape **B**   shape **C**

a   Is shape **A** an **equilateral triangle**?

Explain your answer.

b   Is shape **B** a **kite**?

Explain your answer.

c   Is shape **C** a **square**?

Explain your answer.

This chapter is going to show you

- How to find percentages and use them to compare proportions
- How to work out ratio, leading into simple direct proportion
- How to solve problems using ratio

What you should already know

- How to find equivalent fractions, percentages and decimals
- How to find multiples of 10% of a quantity
- Division facts from tables up to 10×10

Percentages

One of these labels is from a packet of porridge oats. The other is from a toffee cake.

Compare the percentages of protein, carbohydrates, fat and fibre.

PORRIDGE OATS	
Typical values	**per 100 g**
Energy	1555 kJ/ 372 kcal
Protein	7.5 g
Carbohydrates	71 g
Fat	6.0 g
Fibre	6.0 g
Sodium	0.3 g

TOFFEE CAKE	
Typical values	**per 100 g**
Energy	1421 kJ/ 340 kcal
Protein	2.9 g
Carbohydrates	39.1 g
Fat	19.1 g
Fibre	0.3 g
Sodium	0.2 g

Example 12.1 ▷ Without using a calculator find: **a**   12% of £260   **b**   39% of 32

a $12\% = 10\% + 1\% + 1\%$, so 12% of £260 = $26 + 2.6 + 2.6 = £31.20$

b $39\% = 10\% + 10\% + 10\% + 10\% - 1\%$,
so 39% of 32 = $4 \times 3.2 - 0.32 = 12.8 - 0.32 = 12.48$

Example 12.2 ▷ Work out: **a**   6% of £190   **b**   63% of 75 eggs

a $(6 \div 100) \times 190 = £11.40$

b $(63 \div 100) \times 75 = 47.25 = 47$ eggs

Example 12.3 ▷ Which is greater, 42% of 560 or 62% of 390?

$(42 \div 100) \times 560 = 235.2$ $(62 \div 100) \times 390 = 241.8$

62% of 390 is greater.

Exercise 12A

1 Without using a calculator, work out each of these.

a 12% of 320   b 49% of 45   c 31% of 260   d 18% of 68

e 11% of 12   f 28% of 280   g 52% of 36   h 99% of 206

2 Work out each of these.

a 13% of £560   b 46% of 64 books   c 73% of 190 chairs

d 34% of £212   e 64% of 996 pupils   f 57% of 120 buses

g 37% of 109 plants   h 78% of 345 bottles   i 62% of 365 days

j 93% of 2564 people   k 54% of 456 fish   l 45% of £45

m 65% of 366 eggs   n 7% of £684   o 9% of 568 chickens

3 Which is bigger in the following?

a 45% of 68 or 34% of 92?   b 22% of £86 or 82% of £26

c 28% of 79 or 69% of 31   d 32% of 435 or 43% of 325

4 Write down or work out the equivalent percentage and decimal to each of these fractions.

a $\frac{2}{5}$ b $\frac{1}{4}$ c $\frac{3}{8}$ d $\frac{11}{20}$ e $\frac{21}{25}$

5 Write down or work out the equivalent percentage and fraction to each of these decimals.

a 0.1   b 0.75   c 0.34   d 0.85   e 0.31

6 Write down or work out the equivalent fraction and decimal to each of these percentages.

a 15%   b 62.5%   c 8%   d 66.6%   e 80%

7 Javid scores 17 out of 25 on a maths test, 14 out of 20 on a science test and 33 out of 50 on an English test. Work out each score as a percentage.

8 Arrange these numbers in order of increasing size.

a 21%, $\frac{6}{25}$, 0.2   b 0.39, 38%, $\frac{3}{8}$ c $\frac{11}{20}$, 54%, 0.53

Extension Work

The pie chart shows the percentage of each constituent of the toffee cake given in the label on page 150.

Draw a pie chart to show the percentage of each constituent of the porridge oats given on the same page.

Obtain labels from a variety of cereals and other food items. Draw a pie chart for each of them.

What types of food have the most fat? What types of food have the most energy?

Is there a connection between the energy of food and the fat and carbohydrate content?

- Protein
- Carbohydrates
- Fat
- Fibre
- Sodium

Ratio and proportion

Look at the fish tank. There are three types of fish – plain, striped and spotted.

What proportion of the fish are plain? What proportion are striped? What proportion are spotted?

What is the ratio of plain fish to striped fish?

What is the ratio of striped fish to spotted fish?

What is the ratio of plain fish to striped fish?

Proportion is a way of comparing the parts of a quantity to the whole quantity.

Example 12.4 ▷ What proportion of this metre rule is shaded? What is the ratio of the shaded part to the unshaded part?

40 cm out of 100 cm are shaded. This is 40% (or 0.4 or $\frac{2}{5}$). The ratio of shaded to unshaded is $40:60 = 2:3$.

Example 12.5 ▷ A fruit drink is made by mixing 20 cl of orange juice with 60 cl of pineapple juice. What is the proportion of orange juice in the drink?

Total volume of drink is $20 + 60 = 80$ cl.

The proportion of orange is 20 out of $80 = \frac{20}{80} = \frac{1}{4}$.

Example 12.6 ▷ Another fruit drink is made by mixing orange juice and grapefruit juice. The proportion of orange is 40%. 60 cl of orange juice is used. What proportion of grapefruit is used? How much grapefruit juice is used?

The proportion of grapefruit is $100\% - 40\% = 60\%$. Now $40\% = 60$ cl, so $10\% = 15$ cl. So, $60\% = 90$ cl of grapefruit juice.

Example 12.7 ▷ Five pens cost £3.25. How much do 8 pens cost?

First, work out cost of 1 pen: £3.25 ÷ 5 = £0.65
So, 8 pens cost $8 \times £0.65 = £5.20$.

1 Three bars of soap cost £1.80. How much would:

    a 12 bars cost?

    b 30 bars cost?

2 These are the ingredients to make four pancakes.

    a How much of each ingredient will be needed to make 12 pancakes?

    b How much of each ingredient will be needed to make six pancakes?

> 1 egg
> 3 ounces of plain flour
> 5 fluid ounces of milk

3 For each of these metre rules:

    i What proportion of the rule is shaded?

    ii What is the ratio of the shaded part to the unshaded part?

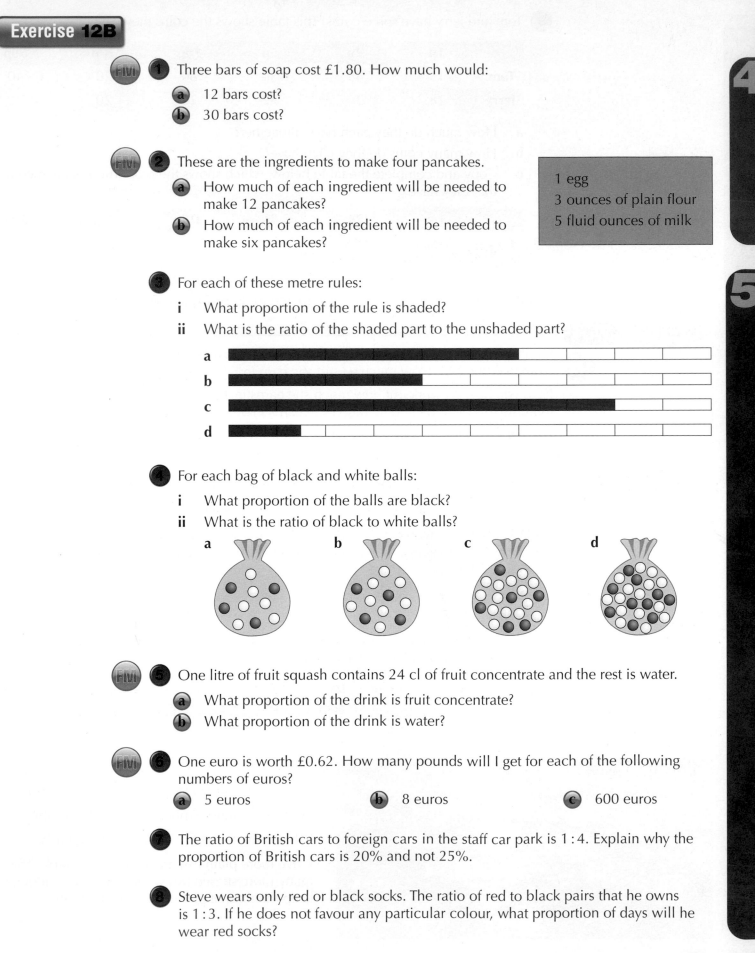

4 For each bag of black and white balls:

    i What proportion of the balls are black?

    ii What is the ratio of black to white balls?

5 One litre of fruit squash contains 24 cl of fruit concentrate and the rest is water.

    a What proportion of the drink is fruit concentrate?

    b What proportion of the drink is water?

6 One euro is worth £0.62. How many pounds will I get for each of the following numbers of euros?

    a 5 euros   **b** 8 euros   **c** 600 euros

7 The ratio of British cars to foreign cars in the staff car park is 1 : 4. Explain why the proportion of British cars is 20% and not 25%.

8 Steve wears only red or black socks. The ratio of red to black pairs that he owns is 1 : 3. If he does not favour any particular colour, what proportion of days will he wear red socks?

9 Tom and Jerry have some coins. This table shows the coins they have.

	1p	2p	5p	10p	20p	50p
Tom	15	45	50	80	20	40
Jerry	18	36	72	24	20	30

a How much do they each have altogether?

b How many coins do they each have?

c Copy and complete the table below, which shows the proportion of each coin that they have.

	1p	2p	5p	10p	20p	50p
Tom	6%	18%				
Jerry						

d Add up the proportions for Tom and for Jerry. Explain your answer.

Extension Work

Direct proportion can be used to solve problems such as: In 6 hours, a woman earns £42. How much would she earn in 5 hours?

First, you have to work out how much she earns in 1 hour: 42 ÷ 6 = £7. Then multiply this by 5 to get how much she earns in 5 hours: 5 × £7 = £35.

Answer the following questions but be careful! Two of them are trick questions.

1 3 kg of sugar cost £1.80. How much do 4 kg of sugar cost?

2 A man can run 10 km in 40 minutes. How long does he take to run 12 km?

3 In two days my watch loses 20 seconds. How much time does it lose in a week?

4 It takes me 5 seconds to dial the 10 digit number of a friend who lives 100 km away. How long does it take me to dial the 10 digit number of a friend who lives 200 miles away?

5 A jet aircraft with 240 people on board takes 2 h 30 min to fly 1000 km. How long would the same aircraft take to fly 1500 km when it had only 120 people on board?

Calculating ratios and proportions

The fish have been breeding!

What is the ratio of striped fish to spotted fish?

What is the ratio of plain fish to spotted fish?

What is the ratio of plain fish to striped fish?

If five more plain fish are added to the tank, how many more striped fish would have to be added to keep the ratio of plain to striped the same?

Example 12.8 ▷

Reduce the following ratios to their simplest form: **a** 4:6   **b** 5:25

a   The highest common factor of 4 and 6 is 2. So, divide 2 into both values, giving 4:6 = 2:3.

b   The highest common factor of 5 and 25 is 5. So, divide 5 into both values, giving 5:25 = 1:5.

Example 12.9 ▷

A fruit drink is made by mixing 20 cl of orange juice with 60 cl of pineapple juice. What is the ratio of orange juice to pineapple juice?

Orange:pineapple = 20:60 = 1:3 (cancel by 20).

Example 12.10 ▷

Another fruit drink is made by mixing orange juice and grapefruit juice in the ratio 2:5. 60 cl of orange juice are used. How much grapefruit juice is needed?

The problem is 60:? = 2:5. You will see that, instead of cancelling, you need to multiply by 30. So, 2:5 = 60:150.

So, 150 cl of grapefruit juice will be needed.

Exercise 12C

1 Reduce each of the following ratios to its simplest form.

a 4:8	**b** 3:9	**c** 2:10	**d** 9:12	**e** 5:20	**f** 8:10
g 4:6	**h** 10:15	**i** 2:14	**j** 4:14	**k** 6:10	**l** 25:30

2 Write down the ratio of shaded:unshaded from each of these metre rules.

a

b

c

3 There are 300 lights on a Christmas tree. 120 are white, 60 are blue, 45 are green and the rest are yellow.

a   Write down the percentage of each colour.

b   Write down each of the following ratios in its simplest form.

   i   white:blue

   ii   blue:green

   iii   green:yellow

   iv   white:blue:green:yellow

4 To make jam, Josh uses strawberries to preserving sugar in the ratio 3 cups : 1 cup.

   a   How many cups of each will he need to make 20 cups of jam altogether?

   b   If he has 12 cups of strawberries, how many cups of sugar will he need?

   c   If he has $2\frac{1}{2}$ cups of sugar, how many cups of strawberries will he need?

Proportion can be used to solve 'best buy' problems.

For example: A large tin of dog food costs 96p and contains 500 grams. A small tin costs 64p and contains 300 grams. Which tin is the better value? For each tin, work out how much 1 gram costs.

Large tin: 500 ÷ 96 = 5.2 grams per penny.
Small tin: 300 ÷ 64 = 4.7 grams per penny. So, the large tin is the better buy.

1   A bottle of shampoo costs £2.62 and contains 30 cl. A different bottle of the same shampoo costs £1.50 and contains 20 cl. Which is the better buy?

2   A large roll of Sellotape has 25 metres of tape and costs 75p. A small roll of Sellotape has 15 metres of tape and costs 55p. Which roll is better value?

3   A pad of A4 paper costs £1.10 and has 120 sheets. A thicker pad of A4 paper costs £1.50 and has 150 sheets. Which pad is the better buy?

4   A small tin of peas contains 250 grams and costs 34p. A large tin costs 70p and contains 454 grams. Which tin is the better buy?

Solving problems

A painter has a 5-litre can of blue paint and 3 litres of yellow paint in a 5-litre can (Picture 1).

Picture 1   **Picture 2**   **Picture 3**

He pours 2 litres of blue paint into the other can (Picture 2) and mixes it thoroughly.

He then pours 1 litre from the second can back into the first can (Picture 3) and mixes it thoroughly.

How much blue paint is in the first can now?

Example 12.11 ▶   Divide £150 in the ratio 1 : 5.

There are 1 + 5 = 6 portions. This gives £150 ÷ 6 = £25 per portion. So one share of the £150 is 1 × 25 = £25, and the other share is 5 × £25 = £125.

Example 12.12 ▶   Two-fifths of a packet of bulbs are daffodils. The rest are tulips. What is the ratio of daffodils to tulips?

Ratio is $\frac{2}{5} : \frac{3}{5}$ = 2 : 3.

Exercise 12D

 1 Divide £100 in the ratio:

     a   2:3   **b**   1:9   **c**   3:7   **d**   1:3   **e**   9:11

2 There are 350 pupils in a primary school. The ratio of girls to boys is 3:2. How many boys and girls are there in the school?

3 Freda has 120 CDs. The ratio of pop CDs to dance CDs is 5:7. How many of each type of CD are there?

4 James is saving 50p coins and £1 coins. He has 75 coins. The ratio of 50p coins to £1 coins is 7:8. How much money does he have altogether?

5 Mr Smith has 24 calculators in a box. The ratio of ordinary calculators to scientific calculators is 5:1. How many of each type of calculator does he have?

6 An exam consists of three parts. A mental test, a non-calculator paper and a calculator paper. The ratio of marks for each is 1:3:4. The whole exam is worth 120 marks. How many marks does each part of the exam get?

7 **a** There are 15 bottles on the wall. The ratio of green bottles to brown bottles is 1:4. How many green bottles are there on the wall?

     b One green bottle accidentally falls. What is the ratio of green to brown bottles now?

8 **a** Forty-nine trains pass through Barnsley station each day. They go to Huddersfield or Leeds in the ratio 3:4. How many trains go to Huddersfield?

     b One day, due to driver shortages, six of the Huddersfield trains are cancelled and three of the Leeds trains are cancelled. What is the ratio of Huddersfield trains to Leeds trains that day?

Extension **Work**

Uncle Fred has decided to give his nephew and niece, Jack and Jill, £100 between them. He decides to split the £100 in the ratio of their ages. Jack is 4 and Jill is 6.

a How much do each get?

b The following year he does the same thing with another £100. How much do each get now?

c He continues to give them £100 shared in the ratio of their ages for another 8 years. How much will each get each year?

d After the 10 years, how much of the £1000 given in total will Jack have? How much will Jill have?

LEVEL BOOSTER

5 I can write down and simplify ratios.
I can calculate a percentage of a quantity.
I know the link between a proportion and a fraction, decimal or percentage.

6 I can use percentages to draw pie charts.
I can divide a quantity in a given ratio.

1 *2000 Paper 1*

The table shows some percentages of amounts of money.

Use the table to work out:

	£10	£30	£45
5%	50p	£1.50	£2.25
10%	£1	£3	£4.50

a 15% of £30 = ...

b £6.75 = 15% of ......

c £3.50 = ... % of £10

d 25p = 5% of ......

2 *2000 Paper 2*

Calculate: **a**   8% of £26.50   **b** $12\frac{1}{2}$% of £98

3 *2005 Paper 1*

a Copy and complete the sentences.

... out of 10 is the same as **70%**

10 out of 20 is the same as **...%**

b Copy and complete the sentence.

... out of ... is the same as **5%**

Now copy and complete the sentence using **different** numbers.

... out of ... is the same as **5%**

4 *2006 Paper 1*

a Work out the missing values.

10% of 84 = ...   5% of 84 = ... $2\frac{1}{2}$% of 84 = ...

a The cost of a CD player is £84 **plus** $17\frac{1}{2}$% tax.

What is the **total** cost of the CD player?

You can use part **a** to help you.

5 *2007 Paper 1*

a In this design, the ratio of **grey to black** is **3 : 1**.

What **percentage** of the design is **black**?

b In this design, **60%** is **grey** and the rest is black.

What is the ratio of **grey to black**?

Write your ratio in its simplest form.

6 *2005 Paper 2*

The screens of widescreen and standard televisions look different. They have different proportions.

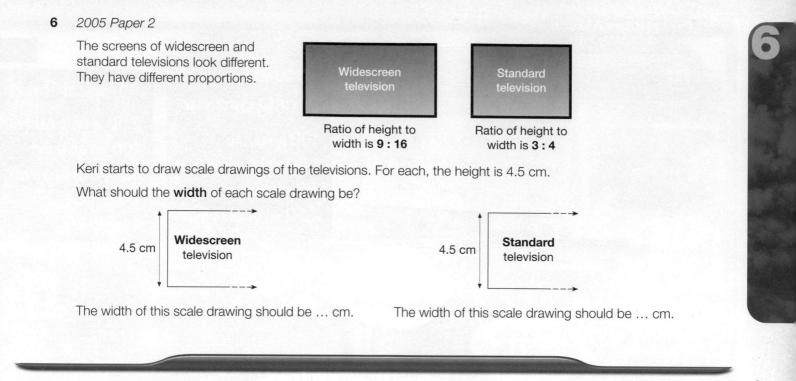

Keri starts to draw scale drawings of the televisions. For each, the height is 4.5 cm.

What should the **width** of each scale drawing be?

4.5 cm | **Widescreen** television

4.5 cm | **Standard** television

The width of this scale drawing should be … cm.   The width of this scale drawing should be … cm.

Smoothie bar

Small	250 ml	£2.50
Medium	400 ml	£3
Large	600 ml	£4

Fruity Surprise
100 g mango
50 g strawberries
75 g bananas
250 ml orange juice

Tropical Fruit
250 g tropical fruit
100 ml yoghurt
85 g raspberries
$\frac{1}{2}$ lime juice
1 tsp honey

To make a small smoothie:
Use 62.5% of the ingredients in the medium recipe.

To make a large smoothie:
Just add 200 ml of fruit juice or milk.

1 Work out the recipe for a small Fruity Surprise.

2 Work out the recipe for a large Chocolate.

3 Work out how many medium Breakfast Boosts can be made with 12 kg of strawberries, 6 litres of milk and 120 bananas. What extras would be needed to make 120 Breakfast Boosts?

6 What proportion of a medium Fruity Surprise is orange juice?

7 I am buying 15 small smoothies. They are Tropical Fruit and Breakfast Boost in the ratio 2 : 3. How many of each type am I buying?

8 If I buy one smoothie of each size, how much will I save using the offer?

Child trust fund

Use the information in the child trust funds key to answer the following questions

Child trust fund

- Children born on or after 1 September 2002 get a £250 voucher from the government to start their child trust fund account.
- They get a further payment of £250 from the government on their seventh birthday.
- If the household income is below the Child Tax Credit income threshold they get an additional £250 with **each** payment.
- Parents, relatives and friends can contribute a maximum of £1200 a year between them to the fund.
- All interest or earnings on the account is tax-free.
- The child (and no-one else) can withdraw the money in the fund when they are 18.
- Money cannot be taken out of the account until the child is 18.

Average annual growth 3%										
		Average annual investment								
		0	150	300	450	600	750	900	1050	1200
Potential amount in account after years shown	1	258	408	558	708	858	1008	1158	1308	1458
	7	565	1714	2864	4013	5162	6312	7461	8611	9760
	13	675	3017	5360	7703	10045	12388	14731	17073	19416
	18	782	4294	7806	11319	14831	18343	21855	25367	28879

Average annual growth 6%										
		Average annual investment								
		0	150	300	450	600	750	900	1050	1200
Potential amount in account after years shown	1	265	415	565	715	865	1015	1165	1315	1465
	7	641	1900	3159	4418	5677	6936	8195	9454	10714
	13	909	3741	6574	9406	12238	15071	17903	20735	23568
	18	1217	5852	10488	15124	19760	24396	29032	33668	38303

1
  a What is 3% of £250?
  b What is 6% of £250?

2 Would children starting school at the age of 5 in September 2008 have a child trust fund? Explain your answer.

3 If the parents of a child decided to invest £500 and the grandparents invest £250 per year in the trust fund, what is the maximum amount the aunt could invest?

4 If a child lived in a household where the income was below the Child Tax Credit limit and no extra investment was made into the fund, explain why there would be approximately £1564 in the trust fund after 18 years.

5 A family has an income below the Child Tax Credit limit. They invest an average of £150 in the child trust fund at an average growth rate of 3%. Approximately how much will be in the account when the child is 18?

6 Look at the amounts in the accounts after 1 year.
  a By how much do the amounts increase for both the average growth rates of 3% and 6%?
  b How much would be in the account after 1 year if the average growth rate is 3% and the amount invested is £75?
  c How much would be in the account after 1 year if the average growth rate is 6% and the amount invested is £675?

7 At an average growth rate of 3%, the amount in the trust fund at 18 for an average investment of £600 is £15 000 to the nearest £1000 and for an average annual investment of £750 is £18 000 to the nearest £1000.

Approximately how much would be in the fund at 18 for an average growth of 3% and an annual investment of £700?

8 At an average growth rate of 3% and the maximum annual investment of £1200 the account would have £29 000 to the nearest £1000 at age 18.

At an average growth rate of 6% and the maximum annual investment of £1200 the account would have £38 000 to the nearest £1000 at age 18.

  a What is the difference between £38 000 and £29 000?
  b Use your answer to a to estimate the amount in an account at age 18 with the maximum investment of £1200 and an average annual growth rate of 4%.

171

④ Write down the order of rotational symmetry for each of the shapes below.

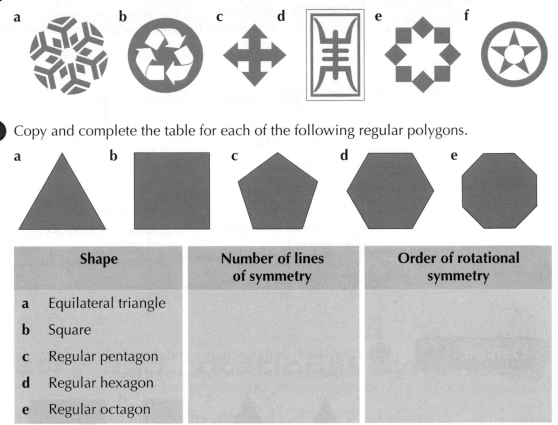

a   b   c   d   e   f

⑤ Copy and complete the table for each of the following regular polygons.

a   b   c   d   e

	Shape	Number of lines of symmetry	Order of rotational symmetry
a	Equilateral triangle		
b	Square		
c	Regular pentagon		
d	Regular hexagon		
e	Regular octagon		

What do you notice?

Extension Work

1 **Symmetry squares**

Two squares can be put together along their sides to make a shape that has line symmetry.

Three squares can be put together along their sides to make 2 different shapes that have line symmetry.

Investigate how many different symmetrical arrangements there are for four squares. What about five squares?

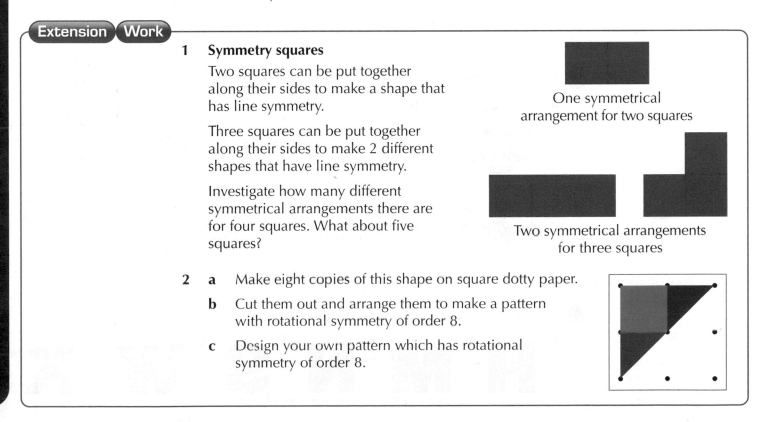

One symmetrical arrangement for two squares

Two symmetrical arrangements for three squares

2 a Make eight copies of this shape on square dotty paper.

b Cut them out and arrange them to make a pattern with rotational symmetry of order 8.

c Design your own pattern which has rotational symmetry of order 8.

Reflections

The picture shows an L-shape reflected in a mirror.

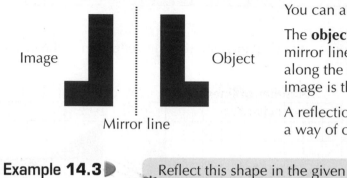

Image   Object

Mirror line

You can also draw the picture without the mirror, as here.

The **object** is reflected in the mirror line to give the **image**. The mirror line becomes a line of symmetry. So, if the paper is folded along the mirror line, the object will fit exactly over the image. The image is the same distance from the mirror line as the object.

A reflection is an example of a **transformation**. A transformation is a way of changing the position or the size of a shape.

Example 14.3 ▷ Reflect this shape in the given mirror line.

Notice that the image is the same size as the object, and that the mirror line becomes a line of symmetry.

Example 14.4 ▷ Triangle A′B′C′ is the reflection of triangle ABC in the given mirror line.

When we change the position of a shape, we sometimes use the term **map**. Here we could write:

△ABC is mapped onto △A′B′C′ by a reflection in the mirror line.

Notice that the line joining A to A′ is perpendicular to the mirror line. This is true for all corresponding points on the object and the image. Also, all corresponding points on the object and image are at the same perpendicular distance from the mirror line.

Example 14.5 ▷ Reflect this rectangle in the mirror line shown.

Use tracing paper to check the reflection.

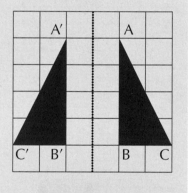

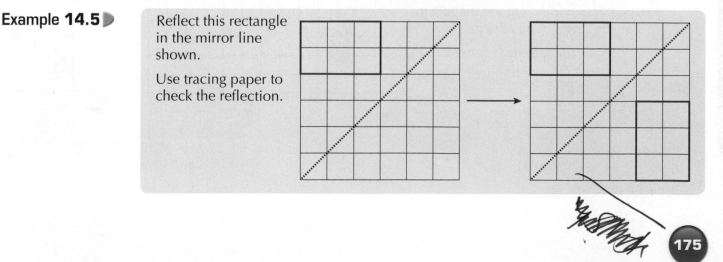

Exercise 14B

1 Copy each of these diagrams onto squared paper and draw its reflection in the given mirror line.

a   b   c   d

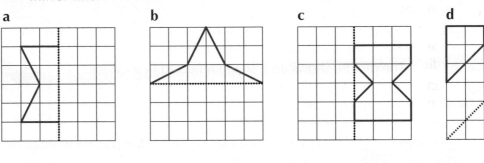

2 Copy each of these shapes onto squared paper and draw its reflection in the given mirror line.

a   b   c   d

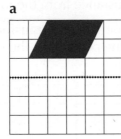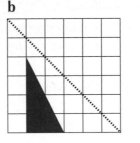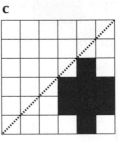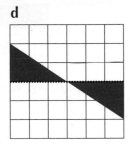

3 The points A(1, 2), B(2, 5), C(4, 4) and D(6, 1) are shown on the grid.

  a Copy the grid onto squared paper and plot the points A, B, C and D. Draw the mirror line.

  b Reflect the points in the mirror line and label them A′, B′, C′ and D′.

  c Write down the coordinates of the image points.

  d The point E(12, 6) is mapped onto E′ by a reflection in the mirror line. What are the coordinates of E′?

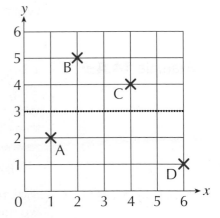

Extension Work

  1 a Copy the diagram onto squared paper and reflect the triangle in the series of parallel mirrors.

     b Make up your own patterns using a series of parallel mirrors.

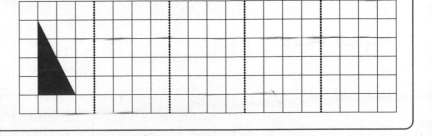

2 **a** Copy the grid onto squared paper and draw the triangle ABC. Write down the coordinates of A, B and C.

b Reflect the triangle in the *x*-axis. Label the vertices of the image A′, B′ and C′. What are the coordinates of A′, B′ and C′?

c Reflect triangle A′B′C′ in the *y*-axis. Label the vertices of this image A″, B″ and C″. What are the coordinates of A″, B″ and C″?

d Reflect triangle A″B″C″ in the *x*-axis. Label the vertices A‴, B‴ and C‴. What are the coordinates of A‴B‴C‴?

e Describe the reflection that maps triangle A‴B‴C‴ onto triangle ABC.

3 Use ICT software, such as LOGO, to reflect shapes in mirror lines.

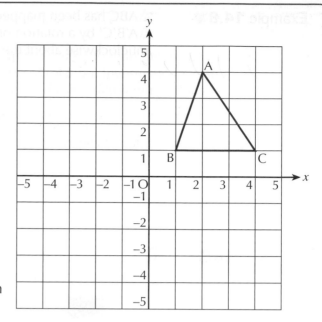

Rotations

Another type of transformation in geometry is **rotation**.

To describe the rotation of a 2-D shape, three facts must be known:

- **Centre of rotation** – this is the point about which the shape rotates.
- **Angle of rotation** – this is usually 90° ($\frac{1}{4}$ turn), 180° ($\frac{1}{2}$ turn) or 270° ($\frac{3}{4}$ turn).
- **Direction of rotation** – this is clockwise or anticlockwise.

When you rotate a shape, it is a good idea to use tracing paper.

As with reflections, the original shape is called the object, and the rotated shape is called the image.

Example 14.6 ▷ The flag is rotated through 90° clockwise about the point X.

Notice that this is the same as rotating the flag through 270° anticlockwise about the point X.

Object

Image

Example 14.7 ▷ This right-angled triangle is rotated through 180° clockwise about the point X.

Notice that this triangle can be rotated either clockwise or anticlockwise when turning through 180°.

Exercise 14D

1 Describe each of the following translations:

   a from A to B

   b from A to C

   c from A to D

   d from A to E

   e from B to D

   f from C to E

   g from D to E

   h from E to A

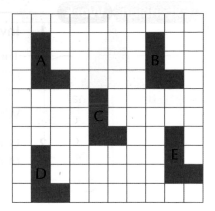

2 Copy the triangle ABC onto squared paper. Label it P.

   a Write down the coordinates of the vertices of triangle P.

   b Translate triangle P 6 units left and 2 units down. Label the new triangle Q.

   c Write down the coordinates of the vertices of triangle Q.

   d Translate triangle Q 5 units right and 4 units down. Label the new triangle R.

   e Write down the coordinates of the vertices of triangle R.

   f Describe the translation which maps triangle R onto triangle P.

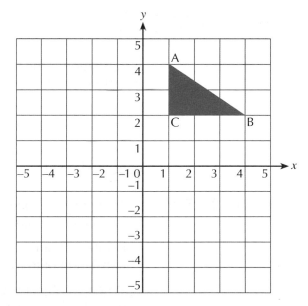

Extension **Work**

1 Use squared dotty paper or a pin-board for this investigation.

   a How many different translations of the triangle are possible on this 3 by 3 grid?

   b How many different translations of this triangle are possible on a 4 by 4 grid?

   c Investigate the number of translations that are possible on any size grid.

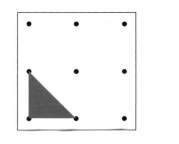

2 Combining transformations

Copy the following triangles A, B, C, D, E, and F onto a square grid.

a Find a single transformation that will map:

i A onto B	**ii** E onto F
iii B onto E	**iv** C onto B

b Find a combination of two transformations that will map:

i A onto C	**ii** B onto F
iii F onto D	**iv** B onto E

c Find other examples of combined transformations for different pairs of triangles.

3 Use ICT software, such as LOGO, to transform shapes by using various combinations of reflections.

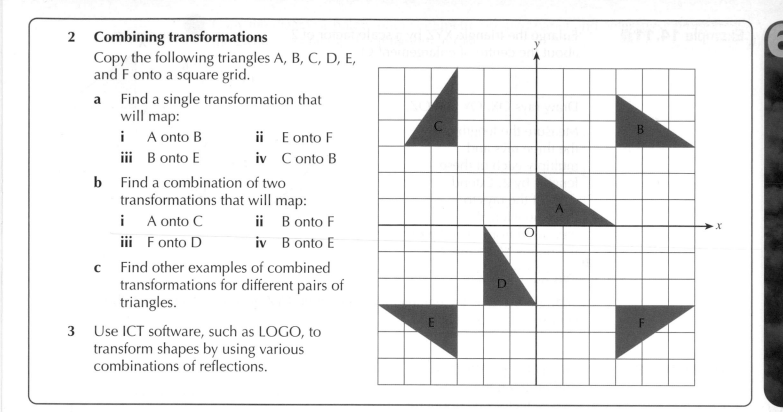

Enlargements

The three transformations you have met so far: reflections, rotations and translations, have not changed the size of the object. You are now going to look at a transformation that does change the size of an object: **an enlargement**.

The diagram below shows triangle ABC enlarged to give triangle A'B'C'.

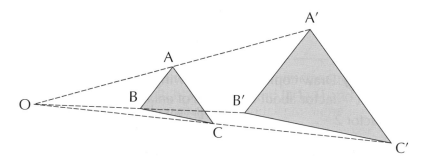

All the sides of triangle A'B'C' are twice as long as the sides of triangle ABC. Notice also that OA' = 2 × OA, OB' = 2 × OB and OC' = 2 × OC.

We say that triangle ABC has been enlarged by a scale factor of 2 about the centre of enlargement O to give the image triangle A'B'C'. The dotted lines are called the guidelines, or rays, for the enlargement. To enlarge a shape we need: a centre of enlargement and a scale factor.

4 I can reflect shapes in a mirror line.

5 I can find the order of rotational symmetry of a 2-D shape.

I can rotate 2-D shapes about a centre of rotation.

I can translate 2-D shapes.

6 I can identify all the symmetries of 2-D shapes.

I can transform 2-D shapes by a combination of reflections, rotations or translations.

I can enlarge 2-D shapes by a scale factor.

National Test questions

1 *2003 4–6 Paper 1*

I have a square grid and two rectangles.

grid   two rectangles

I make a pattern with the grid and the two rectangles:

The pattern has **no** lines of symmetry.

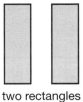

a Put both rectangles on the grid to make a pattern with **two** lines of symmetry.

You must **shade** the rectangles.

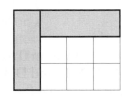

b Put both rectangles on the grid to make a pattern with **only one** line of symmetry.

You must **shade** the rectangles.

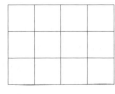

c Put both rectangles on the grid to make a pattern with **rotation** symmetry of **order 2**.

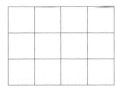

2 *1999 Paper 1*

Write the letter of each shape in the correct space in a copy of the table. You may use a mirror or tracing paper to help you. The letters for the first two shapes have been written for you.

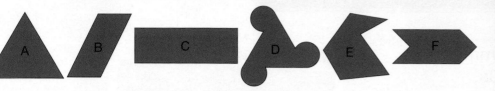

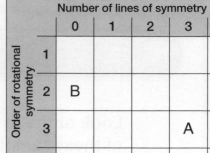

	Number of lines of symmetry			
Order of rotational symmetry	**0**	**1**	**2**	**3**
1				
2	B			
3				A

3 *2005 4–6 Paper 1*

The shapes shown right are drawn on square grids.

The diagrams show a rectangle that is rotated, then rotated again.

The centre of rotation is marked ●.

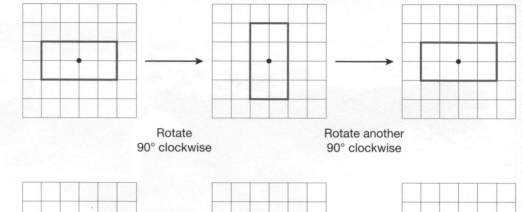

Rotate 90° clockwise

Rotate another 90° clockwise

Copy and complete the diagrams shown right to show the triangle when it is rotated, then rotated again.

The centre of rotation is marked ●.

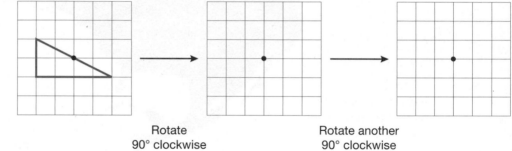

Rotate 90° clockwise

Rotate another 90° clockwise

4 *2002 Paper 2*

The grid shows an arrow.

On a copy of the grid, draw an **enlargement** of **scale factor 2** of the arrow.

Use **point C** as the centre of enlargement.

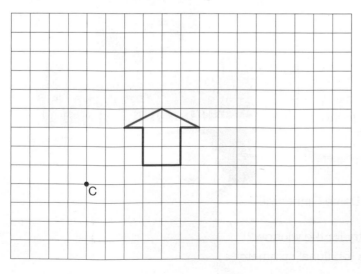

Landmark spotting

Look at the symmetry of these famous landmarks

d The Angel of the North

a Notre Dame Cathedral

1 How many lines of symmetry does each picture have?

Draw sketches to show the lines of symmetry.

2 The picture for some of the buildings will have a different number of lines if the picture was taken directly from above. We call this the aerial view.

How many lines of symmetry would a picture of the Eiffel Tower have from an aerial view?

Draw a sketch to show the lines of symmetry.

Explain why it may not be possible to do this for the aerial views of the other buildings.

3 Look carefully at the window of Notre Dame Cathedral. It has rotation symmetry.

What is the order of rotational symmetry for the window?

Design a window of your own that has rotational symmetry.

c Millennium Dome

4 Look at the buildings in the town where you live.

Do any of them or parts of them have symmetry?

Look particularly at churches, Georgian buildings and modern office blocks.

Make sketches of anything you find and comment on the symmetry.

b Taj Mahal

e Eiffel Tower

f Petronas Towers

5 Can you find any other famous landmarks that have symmetry? Use the Internet to help.

Make a list of all the buildings that you find.

3 Look at each set of data and give a reason why the chosen average is suitable or not.

a	2, 3, 5, 7, 8, 10	Mean
b	0, 1, 2, 2, 2, 4, 6	Mode
c	1, 4, 7, 8, 10, 11, 12	Median
d	2, 3, 6, 7, 10, 10, 10	Mode
e	2, 2, 2, 2, 4, 6, 8	Median
f	1, 2, 4, 6, 9, 30	Mean

4 Look at each set of data and decide which average is the most suitable. Explain your answer.

a	1, 2, 4, 7, 9, 10
b	1, 10, 10, 10, 10
c	1, 1, 1, 2, 10
d	1, 3, 5, 6, 7, 10
e	1, 1, 1, 7, 10, 10, 10
f	2, 5, 8, 10, 14

Extension **Work**

Get two different makes of scientific calculator.

Use each of them to generate 100 random digits. (Some calculators give a number such as 0.786 when the random button is pressed. In this case take the three digits after the decimal point as three separate, random numbers. For example: for 0.786, record 7, 8 and 6; for 0.78 (= 0.780), record 7, 8 and 0.)

Work out the mean and the range for each set of numbers. The range should be 9 (smallest digit should be zero and largest 9). The mean should be 4.5.

Which calculator is better at generating random numbers?

Statistical surveys

You are about to carry out your own statistical survey and write a report on your findings.

Once you have chosen a problem to investigate, you will first need to plan how you intend to carry out the survey and decide how you are going to collect your data.

When you have done this, you may want to write down any statements which you want to test and the responses you might expect to receive from your survey. These will be your hypotheses.

Your data may be obtained in one of the following ways.

- A survey of a sample of people. Your sample size should be more than 30. To collect data from your chosen sample, you will need to use a data collection sheet or a questionnaire.
- Carrying out experiments. You will need to keep a record of your observations on a data collection sheet.
- Searching secondary sources. Examples are reference books, newspapers, ICT databases and the Internet.

If you plan to use a data collection sheet, remember the following points:

- Decide what types of data you need to collect.
- Design the layout of your sheet before you start the survey.
- Keep a tally of your results in a table.

If you plan to use a questionnaire, remember the following points:

- Make the questions short and simple.
- Choose questions that require simple responses. For example: Yes, No, Do not know. Or use tick boxes with a set of multichoice answers.
- Avoid personal and embarrassing questions.
- Never ask a leading question designed to get a particular response.

When you have collected all your data, you are ready to write a report on your findings.

Your report should be short and based only on the evidence you have collected. Use statistics, such as the mean, the median, the mode and the range, to help give an overall picture of the facts. Also, use statistical diagrams to illustrate your results and to make them easier to understand. For example, you might draw bar charts, line graphs or pie charts. Try to give a reason why you have chosen to use a particular type of diagram.

To give your report a more professional look, use ICT software to illustrate the data.

Finally, you will need to write a short conclusion based on your evidence. This may require you to refer to your original hypotheses. You should include a reference to any averages you have calculated or to any diagrams you have drawn.

Exercise 15C

Write your own statistical report on one or more of the following problems.

Remember:

- Write down any hypotheses for the problem.
- Decide on your sample size.
- Decide whether you need to use a data collection sheet or a questionnaire.
- Find any relevant averages.
- Illustrate your report with suitable diagrams or graphs, and explain why you have used them.
- Write a short conclusion based on all the evidence.

The data can be collected from people in your class or year group, but it may be possible to collect the data from other sources, friends and family outside school.

 1 The amount of TV young people watch.

 2 The types of sport young people take part in outside school.

3 The musical likes and dislikes of Year 7 pupils.

 4 Investigate the young woman's statement.

> Taller people have a larger head circumference.

 5 'More people are taking holidays abroad this year.' Investigate this statement.

3 You will need a box or a bag containing two red counters, three green counters and five blue counters.

   a Working in pairs, pick a counter from the box and note its colour. Replace it, shake the box and pick another counter. Repeat the experiment 50 times and record your results on a copy of the following frequency table.

Colour	Tally	Frequency
Red		
Green		
Blue		

   Use your results to find the experimental probability of getting:

   i a red counter   **ii** a green counter   **iii** a blue counter

   b Write down the theoretical probability of getting:

   i a red counter   **ii** a green counter   **iii** a blue counter

   c By writing your answers to parts **a** and **b** as decimals, state whether you think the experiment is fair or not.

4 Two fair dice are thrown.

   a Copy and complete the sample space diagram for the total scores.

   b What is the theoretical probability of a double?

   c Design and carry out an experiment to test whether you think the two dice are fair.

   d If you repeated the experiment using more trials, what would you expect to happen to the estimate of probability?

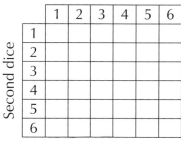

First dice

Second dice

Extension Work

For this activity, you will need to work in pairs or groups.

On a large sheet of paper or card, draw a square measuring 40 cm by 40 cm. Divide into 100 squares, each measuring 4 cm by 4 cm.

- Each person rolls a 2p coin onto the sheet 50 times.
- If the coin lands completely inside a small square, score 1 point.
- If the coin touches or covers any line when it lands, score 0 point.
- The winner is the person who gets the most points.
- Work out the experimental probability of a coin landing completely inside a small square.
- You often see games like this one at fun fairs and village fêtes. Do you think these games are fair?

5 I can compare two distributions using mean and range, then draw conclusions.

I can interpret pie charts.

I can calculate probabilities based on experimental evidence.

6 I can construct pie charts.

I can construct and interpret frequency diagrams.

I can identify all the outcomes from a two-event combination using diagrams or tables.

National Test questions

1 *2005 Paper 2*

Look at this information:

In 1976, a man earned £16 each week.

The pie chart shows how this man spent his money:

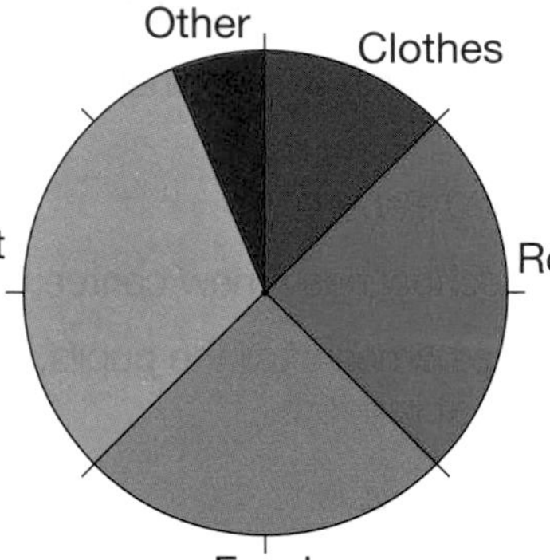

a How much did the man spend on **food** each week?

b Now look at this information:

In 2002, a man earned £400 each week.

This table shows how he spent his money:

Rent	£200
Food	£100
Entertainment	£50
Other	£50

Copy and complete the pie chart to show how the man spent his money.

Remember to **label** each sector of the pie chart.

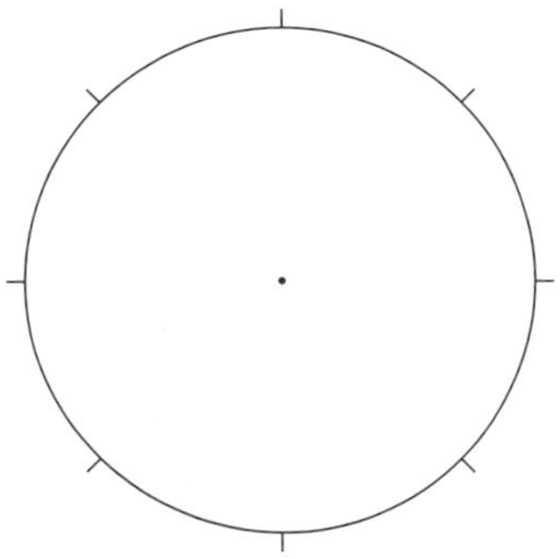

CHAPTER 16

Number **5**

This chapter is going to show you	What you should already know
● How to multiply and divide decimals ● How to use the memory keys on a calculator ● How to use the square root and sign change keys on a calculator ● How to calculate fractions and percentages of quantities	● How to do long and short multiplication and division ● Equivalence of fractions, decimals and percentages ● How to use a calculator efficiently, including the use of brackets

Multiplying decimals

This section will show you how to easily work out the correct number of decimal places in your answer when multiplying with decimals.

Example 16.1 ▷ Work out: **a** 0.8×0.7 **b** 0.02×0.7

a $8 \times 7 = 56$, so $0.\underline{8} \times 0.\underline{7} = 0.\underline{56}$ because the number of decimal places in the answer is always the same as in the original calculation.

b $2 \times 7 = 14$, and there are three decimal places in the original calculation, so $0.02 \times 0.7 = 0.014$.

Notice that a zero has been put in to make-up the correct number of decimal places.

Example 16.2 ▷ Work out: **a** 2000×0.07 **b** $0.06 \times 50\,000$

a $2000 \times 0.07 = 200 \times 0.7 = 20 \times 7 = 140$

If we divide one number by 10 and multiply the other by 10, then their product will remain the same.

b $0.06 \times 50\,000 = 0.6 \times 5000 = 6 \times 500$

These are all equivalent calculations, so the answer is $6 \times 500 = 3000$.

Exercise 16A

1 Without using a calculator, write down the answer to each of these.

a 0.2×0.3	**b** 0.4×0.2	**c** 0.6×0.6	**d** 0.7×0.2
e 0.02×0.4	**f** 0.8×0.04	**g** 0.06×0.1	**h** 0.3×0.03
i 0.7×0.8	**j** 0.07×0.08	**k** 0.9×0.3	**l** 0.006×0.9
m 0.5×0.09	**n** 0.5×0.5	**o** 0.8×0.005	**p** 0.06×0.03

2 Without using a calculator, work out each of these.

a	300×0.8	**b**	0.06×200	**c**	0.6×500	**d**	0.02×600
e	0.03×400	**f**	0.004×500	**g**	0.007×200	**h**	0.002×9000
i	0.005×8000	**j**	200×0.006	**k**	300×0.01	**l**	800×0.06
m	500×0.5	**n**	400×0.05	**o**	300×0.005	**p**	200×0.0005

3 Without using a calculator, work out each of these.

a	$0.006 \times 400 \times 200$	**b**	$0.04 \times 0.06 \times 50\,000$	**c**	$0.2 \times 0.04 \times 300$
d	$300 \times 200 \times 0.08$	**e**	$20 \times 0.008 \times 40$	**f**	$0.1 \times 0.07 \times 2000$

4 Bolts cost £0.06 each. An engineering company orders 20 000 bolts. How much will this cost?

5 A grain of sand weighs 0.006 grams. How much would 500 000 grains weigh?

6 A kilogram of uranium ore contains 0.000002 kg of plutonium.

a How much plutonium is in a tonne of ore?

b In a year, 2 million tonnes of ore are mined. How much plutonium will this give?

Extension Work

1 Work out each of these.

a 0.1×0.1 **b** $0.1 \times 0.1 \times 0.1$ **c** $0.1 \times 0.1 \times 0.1 \times 0.1$

2 Using your answers to **1**, write each of these as a decimal.

a 0.1^5 **b** 0.1^6 **c** 0.1^7 **d** 0.1^{10}

3 Write down the answer to each of these.

a	0.2^2	**b**	0.3^2	**c**	0.4^2	**d**	0.5^2	**e**	0.8^2
f	0.2^3	**g**	0.3^3	**h**	0.4^3	**i**	0.5^3	**j**	0.8^3

Dividing decimals

Example 16.3 ▷ Work out: **a** $0.08 \div 0.2$ **b** $20 \div 0.05$

a Rewrite as equivalent divisions.

$$0.08 \div 0.2 = 0.8 \div 2 = 0.4$$

We have shifted the decimal point in both of the numbers by the same amount, in the same direction.

b Rewrite as equivalent divisions.

$$20 \div 0.05 = 200 \div 0.5 = 2000 \div 5 = 400$$

Exercise 16C

1 Use the memory keys to work out each of the following. Write down any values that you store in the memory.

a $\dfrac{17.8 + 25.6}{14.5 - 8.3}$ b $\dfrac{35.7 - 19.2}{34.9 - 19.9}$ c $\dfrac{16.9 + 23.6}{16.8 - 14.1}$ d $\dfrac{47.2 - 19.6}{11.1 - 8.8}$

e $45.6 - (23.4 - 6.9)$ f $44.8 \div (12.8 - 7.2)$ g $(4 \times 28.8) \div (9.5 - 3.1)$

2 Use the sign change key to enter the first negative number. Then use the calculator to work out the value of each of these.

a $-2 + 3 - 7$ b $-4 - 6 + 8$ c $-6 + 7 - 8 + 2$ d $-5 + 3 - 8 + 9$

3 Use the square root key to work out the following.

a $\sqrt{400}$ b $\sqrt{300}$ c $\sqrt{150}$ d $\sqrt{10}$

4 What happens if you press the sign key twice in succession?

5 If you start with 16 and press the square root key twice in succession, the display shows 2. If you start with 81 and press the square root key twice in succession, the display shows 3.

Explain what numbers are shown in the display.

6 Calculate each of the following **i** using the brackets keys, and **ii** using the memory keys.

Write out the key presses for each. Which method uses fewer key presses?

a $\dfrac{12.9 + 42.9}{23.7 - 14.4}$ b $\dfrac{72.4 - 30.8}{16.85 - 13.6}$ c $25.6 \div (6.7 - 3.5)$

Extension Work

It helps to understand how a calculator works if you can think like a calculator. So, do the following without using a calculator.

You are told what the number in the memory and the number in the display are.

After each series of operations shown below, what number will be in the display and what number will be in the memory? The first one has been done as an example.

	Starting number in display	Starting number in memory	Operations	Final number in display	Final number in memory
	6	10	M+, M+, M+	6	28
a	6	10	Min, M+, M+		
b	6	10	M−, MR		
c	12	5	M+, MR, M+		
d	10	6	M+, M+, M+, MR		
e	10	6	MR, M+, M+		
f	8	8	M−, M+, MR, M+		
g	15	20	M−, M−, MR, M+		
h	10	6	MR, M−		
i	15	0	M+, M+, MR, M+		
j	0	15	M+, M+, MR, M+		

Fractions of quantities

This section is going to help you to revise the rules for working with fractions.

Example 16.7

Find: **a** $\frac{2}{7}$ of £28   **b** $\frac{3}{5}$ of 45 sweets   **c** $1\frac{2}{3}$ of 15 m

a First, find $\frac{1}{7}$ of £28: $28 \div 7 = 4$. So, $\frac{2}{7}$ of £28 $= 2 \times 4 = £8$.

b First, find $\frac{1}{5}$ of 45 sweets: $45 \div 5 = 9$. So, $\frac{3}{5}$ of 45 sweets $= 3 \times 9 = 27$ sweets.

c Either calculate $\frac{2}{3}$ of 15 and add it to 15, or make $1\frac{2}{3}$ into a top-heavy fraction and work out $\frac{5}{3}$ of 15.

$15 \div 3 = 5$, so $\frac{2}{3}$ of 15 = 10. So, $1\frac{2}{3}$ of 15 m = 15 + 10 = 25 m.

$15 \div 3 = 5$, so $\frac{5}{3}$ of 15 = 25 m.

Example 16.8

Find: **a** $7 \times \frac{3}{4}$ **b** $8 \times \frac{2}{3}$ **c** $5 \times 1\frac{3}{5}$

a $7 \times \frac{3}{4} = \frac{21}{4} = 5\frac{1}{4}$

b $8 \times \frac{2}{3} = \frac{16}{3} = 5\frac{1}{3}$

c $5 \times 1\frac{3}{5} = 5 \times \frac{8}{5} = \frac{40}{5} = 8$

Example 16.9

A magazine has 96 pages. $\frac{5}{12}$ of the pages have adverts on them. How many pages have adverts on them?

$\frac{1}{12}$ of 96 = 8. So, $\frac{5}{12}$ of 96 = $5 \times 8 = 40$ pages.

Exercise 16D

1 Find each of these.

a $\frac{2}{3}$ of £27   **b** $\frac{3}{5}$ of 75 kg   **c** $1\frac{2}{3}$ of 18 metres **d** $\frac{4}{9}$ of £18

e $\frac{3}{10}$ of £46   **f** $\frac{5}{8}$ of 840 houses   **g** $\frac{3}{7}$ of 21 litres   **h** $1\frac{2}{5}$ of 45 minutes

i $\frac{5}{6}$ of £63   **j** $\frac{3}{8}$ of 1600 loaves   **k** $1\frac{4}{7}$ of 35 km   **l** $\frac{7}{10}$ of 600 crows

m $\frac{2}{9}$ of £1.26   **n** $\frac{4}{9}$ of 540 children   **o** $\frac{7}{12}$ of 144 miles **p** $3\frac{3}{11}$ of £22

2 Find each of these as a mixed number.

a $5 \times \frac{3}{4}$ **b** $8 \times \frac{2}{7}$ **c** $6 \times 1\frac{2}{3}$ **d** $4 \times \frac{3}{8}$

e $9 \times \frac{1}{4}$ **f** $5 \times 1\frac{5}{6}$ **g** $9 \times \frac{4}{5}$ **h** $7 \times 2\frac{3}{4}$

i $3 \times 3\frac{3}{7}$ **j** $8 \times \frac{2}{11}$ **k** $4 \times 1\frac{2}{7}$ **l** $6 \times \frac{7}{9}$

m $2 \times 3\frac{3}{4}$ **n** $3 \times \frac{7}{10}$ **o** $5 \times 1\frac{3}{10}$ **p** $2 \times 10\frac{5}{8}$

3 A bag of rice weighed 1300 g. $\frac{2}{5}$ of it was used to make a meal. How much was left?

4 Mrs Smith weighed 96 kg. She lost $\frac{3}{8}$ of her weight due to a diet. How much did she weigh after the diet?

⑤ A petrol tank holds 52 litres. $\frac{3}{4}$ is used on a journey. How many litres are left?

⑥ A GCSE textbook has 448 pages. $\frac{3}{28}$ of the pages are the answers. How many pages of answers are there?

⑦ A bar of chocolate weighs $\frac{5}{8}$ of a kilogram. How much do seven bars weigh?

⑧ A Smartie machine produces 1400 Smarties a minute. $\frac{2}{7}$ of them are red. How many red Smarties will the machine produce in an hour?

⑨ A farmer has nine cows. Each cow eats $1\frac{2}{3}$ bales of silage a week. How much do they eat altogether?

⑩ A cake recipe requires $\frac{2}{3}$ of a cup of walnuts. How many cups of walnuts will be needed for five cakes?

Extension Work

This is about dividing fractions by a whole number.

Dividing a fraction by 2 has the same effect as halving the fraction. For example:

$$\frac{2}{7} \div 2 = \frac{2}{7} \times \frac{1}{2} = \frac{1}{7}$$

Work out each of the following as a fraction.

a	$\frac{2}{3} \div 2$	**b**	$\frac{3}{4} \div 2$	**c**	$\frac{4}{5} \div 2$	**d**	$\frac{7}{8} \div 2$
e	$\frac{4}{7} \div 3$	**f**	$\frac{2}{5} \div 5$	**g**	$\frac{3}{8} \div 4$	**h**	$\frac{3}{10} \div 5$
i	$\frac{3}{4} \div 6$	**j**	$\frac{2}{3} \div 3$	**k**	$\frac{2}{11} \div 10$	**l**	$\frac{3}{8} \div 8$
m	$\frac{3}{7} \div 4$	**n**	$\frac{3}{4} \div 5$	**o**	$\frac{7}{8} \div 3$	**p**	$\frac{4}{5} \div 9$

Percentages of quantities

This section will show you how to calculate simple percentages of quantities. This section will also revise the equivalence between fractions, percentages and decimals.

Example 16.10 ▶

Calculate: **a**   15% of £670   **b**   40% of £34

Calculate 10%, then use multiples of this.

a   10% of £670 = £67, 5% = 33.50. So, 15% of £670 = 67 + 33.5 = £100.50.

b   10% of £34 = £3.40. So, 40% of £34 = 4 × 3.40 = £13.60.

Example 16.11 ▷

Write down the equivalent percentage and fraction for each of these decimals.

a 0.6 **b** 0.28

To change a decimal to a percentage, multiply by 100. This gives: **a** 60% **b** 28%

To change a decimal to a fraction, multiply and divide by 10, 100, 1000 as appropriate and cancel if possible. This gives:

a $0.6 = \frac{6}{10} = \frac{3}{5}$ **b** $0.28 = \frac{28}{100} = \frac{7}{25}$

Example 16.12 ▷

Write down the equivalent percentage and decimal for each of these fractions.

a $\frac{7}{20}$ **b** $\frac{9}{25}$

To change a fraction into a percentage, make the denominator 100. This gives:

a $\frac{7}{20} = \frac{35}{100} = 35\%$ **b** $\frac{9}{25} = \frac{36}{100} = 36\%$

To change a fraction into a decimal, divide the top by the bottom, or make into a percentage, then divide by 100. This gives:

a 0.35 **b** 0.36

Example 16.13 ▷

Write down the equivalent decimal and fraction for each of these percentages.

a 95% **b** 26%

To convert a percentage to a decimal, divide by 100. This gives: **a** 0.95 **b** 0.26

To convert a percentage to a fraction, make a fraction over 100 then cancel if possible. This gives:

a $95\% = \frac{95}{100} = \frac{19}{20}$ **b** $26\% = \frac{26}{100} = \frac{13}{50}$

Exercise 16E

1 Calculate each of these.

  a 35% of £340   **b** 15% of £250   **c** 60% of £18   **d** 20% of £14.40

  e 45% of £440   **f** 5% of £45   **g** 40% of £5.60   **h** 25% of £24.40

2 A bus garage holds 50 buses. 34% are single-deckers, the rest are double-deckers.

  a How many single-deckers are there?

  b How many double-deckers are there?

  c What percentage are double-deckers?

3 A Jumbo Jet carries 400 passengers. On one trip, 52% of the passengers were British, 17% were American, 12% were French and the rest were German.

  a How many people of each nationality were on the plane?

  b What percentage were German?

(4) Copy and complete this table.

	a	b	c	d	e	f	g	h	i	j
Decimal	0.45		0.76				0.36			0.85
Fraction	$\frac{9}{20}$	$\frac{3}{5}$			$\frac{4}{25}$			$\frac{3}{50}$		
Percentage	45%		32%		37.5%					65%

(5) Copy the cross-number puzzle. Use the clues to fill it in. Then use the puzzle to fill in the missing numbers in the clues.

Across
1 71% of 300
3 73% of 200
5 107% of 200
8 58% of ......
9 88% of 400

Down
1 96% of ......
2 81% of ......
3 50% of 24
4 25% of 596
6 61% of 200
7 100% of 63

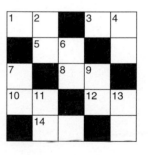

Extension Work

Copy the cross-number puzzle. Work out each percentage.
Then use the puzzle to fill in the missing numbers in the clues.

Across
1   54 out of 200
3   33 out of 50
5   13 out of 25
8   99 out of 100
10 ...... out of 200
12 27 out of 50
14 38 out of 200

Down
2   ...... out of 400
4   134 out of 200
6   ...... out of 300
7   100 out of 400
9   ...... out of 20
11 110 out of 1000
13 23 out of 50

Solving problems

Below are two investigations. Before you start either of these, read the question carefully and think about how you are going to record your results. Show all your working clearly.

Who wants to be a millionaire?

You have won a prize in a lottery. You have a choice of how to take the prize.

You can either:

Take £10 000 in the first year, 10% less (£9000) in the second year, 10% less than the second year's amount (£8100) in the third year, and so on for 10 years.

Or

Take £1000 in the first year, 50% more (£1500) in the second year, 50% more than the second year's amount (£2250) in the third year, and so on for 10 years.

Which would you choose? You will probably need to use a calculator and round off the amounts to the nearest penny.

Would your choice change if the second method gave 40% more each year? Would your choice change if the second method started with £10 000?

 Chocolate bars

Eight children, Alf, Betty, Charles, Des, Ethel, Fred, George and Helen, are lined up outside a room in alphabetical order.

Inside the room are three tables. Each table has eight chairs around it.

On the first table is one chocolate bar, on the second table are two chocolate bars, and on the third table are three chocolate bars.

The children go into the room one at a time and sit at one of the tables. After they are all seated they share out the chocolate bars on the table at which they are seated.

Where should Alf sit to make sure he gets the most chocolate?

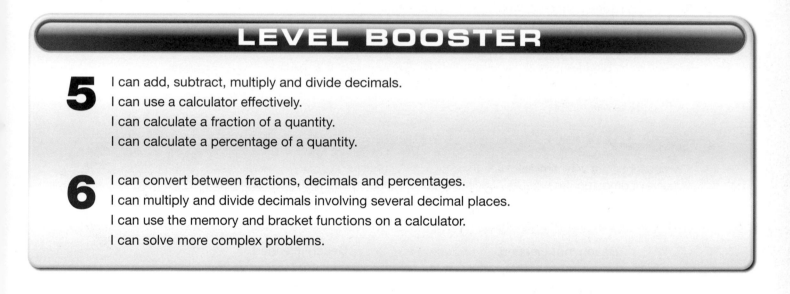

LEVEL BOOSTER

5
I can add, subtract, multiply and divide decimals.
I can use a calculator effectively.
I can calculate a fraction of a quantity.
I can calculate a percentage of a quantity.

6
I can convert between fractions, decimals and percentages.
I can multiply and divide decimals involving several decimal places.
I can use the memory and bracket functions on a calculator.
I can solve more complex problems.

National Test questions

1 *2004 Paper 1*

You can buy a new calculator for **£1.25**.

In 1979 the same type of calculator cost **22 times** as much as it costs now.

How much did the same type of calculator cost in 1979?

Show your working.

2 *2003 Paper 2*

a A glass holds **225 ml.**

An adult needs about **1.8 litres** of water each day to stay healthy.

How many glasses is that?

Show your working.

225 ml

b An adult weighs **80 kg.**

60% of his total mass is water.

What is the mass of the water?

3 *2007 Paper 1*

a Some of the fractions below are **smaller than** $\frac{1}{9}$

Write them down.

$\frac{1}{10}$ $\frac{4}{9}$ $\frac{1}{2}$ $\frac{1}{100}$ $\frac{1}{8}$

b To the nearest per cent, what is $\frac{1}{9}$ as a percentage?

Write down the correct percentage.

0.9%   9%   10%   11%   19%

c Copy and complete the sentence by writing a fraction.

$\frac{1}{9}$ is half of …

4 *2003 Paper 2*

Two beaches are very similar.
A survey compared the number of animals found in one square metre on each beach.

One beach had not been cleaned.
The other beach had been cleaned.

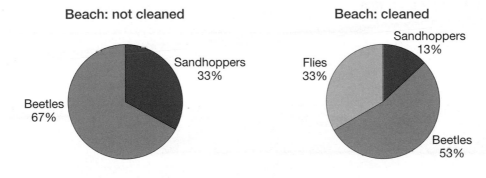

Beach: not cleaned

Sandhoppers 33%
Beetles 67%

Beach: cleaned

Sandhoppers 13%
Flies 33%
Beetles 53%

a The data for the beach that had **not been cleaned** represent **1620** animals.

Copy and complete the table to show how many of each animal were found.

Beach: not cleaned

	Number found
Sandhoppers	
Beetles	
Flies	

b The data for the beach that had been **cleaned** represent **15** animals.

Copy and complete the table to show how many of each animal were found on the clean beach.

Beach: cleaned

	Number found
Sandhoppers	
Beetles	
Flies	

c Cleaning the beach changes the number of animals and the proportions of animals.

Write a sentence to describe **both** these changes.

Running a small business – a group activity

Plan

1 You are setting up a small business to buy materials, make gadgets and sell them for profit.

Facts

2 You have £20 000 to invest in your business.

One machine to produce your gadgets costs £2500.

The machines also cost £500 per week each to maintain.

Each machine can produce 100 gadgets per day but requires two workers to use it.

Workers are paid £400 per week each.

The cost of materials to produce one gadget is £12.

Tax is deducted on any profit made at 15%.

Weekly sales figures

3 The number of sales depends on the selling price. The table shows maximum weekly sales for different selling prices.

Selling price	£18	£19	£20	£21
Maximum number of gadgets that can be sold per week	2000	1500	1000	500

4 To make as much profit as possible at the end of 6 weeks.

5 Try buying different numbers of machines to start with.

Use some of your profits to buy extra machines.

Sell at the highest of the selling prices that you can.

Your **total costs** cannot be greater than the amount of money you have at the start of any week.

An example

6 Here is an example of a week if you buy one machine and employ two workers.

Be careful: If you buy four machines you cannot pay any workers to produce gadgets and will be bankrupt!

Week 1
(£20 000 available to spend)

Cost of machines bought	$1 \times £2500 = £2500$		Income = Selling price × Number of gadgets sold	$500 \times £21 = £10\,500$
Maintenance cost of machines	$1 \times £500 = £500$			
Cost of workers	$2 \times £400 = £800$		Total profit	$£10\,500 - £9800 = £700$
Number of gadgets produced	500		Tax on profit	15% of £700 = £105
Cost of materials	$500 \times £12 = £6000$		**Net profit**	$£700 - £105 = £595$
Total costs	£9800		Balance	$£20\,000 + £595 = 20\,595$

Profit for week 1 = £595
Amount available to spend in week 2 = £20 595

Tessellations

A **tessellation** is a pattern made by fitting together identical shapes without leaving any gaps.

When drawing a tessellation, use a square or a triangular grid, as in the examples below.

To show a tessellation, it is usual to draw up to about ten repeating shapes.

Example **18.3** ▶

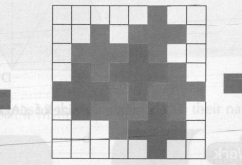

Two different shapes which each make a tessellation on a square grid.

Example **18.4** ▶

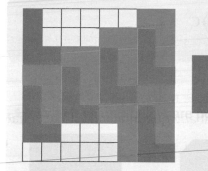

This shape tessellates on a triangular grid.

Example **18.5** ▶

Circles *do not* tessellate.

However you try to fit circles together, there will always be gaps.

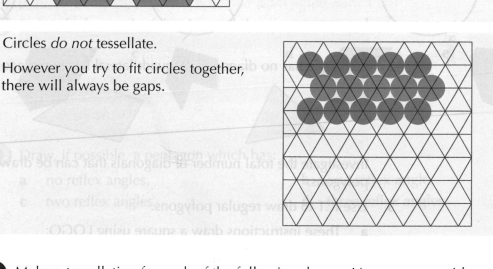

Exercise 18B

1 Make a tessellation for each of the following shapes. Use a square grid.

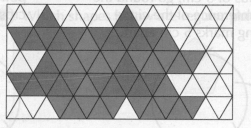

a   b   c   d

2 Make a tessellation for each of the following shapes. Use a triangular grid.

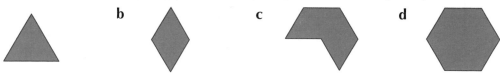

a   b   c   d

1   Design a tessellation of your own. Working in pairs or groups, make an attractive poster to show all your different tessellations.

2   Here is a tessellation which uses curves. Can you design a different curved tessellation?

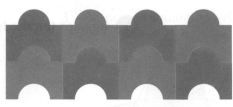

3   Investigate which of the regular polygons will tessellate. Can you find a rule to predict if a regular polygon will tessellate, without having to try it out?

4   Any quadrilateral will tessellate. So, make an irregular quadrilateral tile cut from card. Then use your tile to show how it tessellates.

Can you explain why it is that *any* quadrilateral will tessellate?

Constructing 3-D shapes

A net is a 2-D shape which can be cut out and folded up to make a 3-D shape.

To make the nets overleaf into 3-D shapes you will need the following equipment: a sharp pencil, a ruler, a protractor, a pair of scissors and a glue-stick or sticky tape.

Always score the card along the fold-lines using scissors and a ruler. This makes the card much easier to fold properly.

You can glue the edges together using the tabs or you can just use sticky tape. If you decide to use glue, then always keep one face of the shape free of tabs and glue down this face last.

Example 18.6 ▷

Constructing a square-based pyramid

1   Carefully cut out the net using scissors.

2   Score along each fold-line using a ruler and scissors.

3   Fold along each fold-line and stick the shape together by gluing each tab.

4   The last face to stick down is the one without any tabs.

1 *2000 Paper 1*

The sketch shows the net of a triangular prism.

The net is folded up and glued to make the prism.

a Which edge is tab 1 glued to? On a copy of the diagram, label this edge A.

b Which edge is tab 2 glued to? Label this edge B.

c The corner marked ● meets two other corners. Label these two other corners ●.

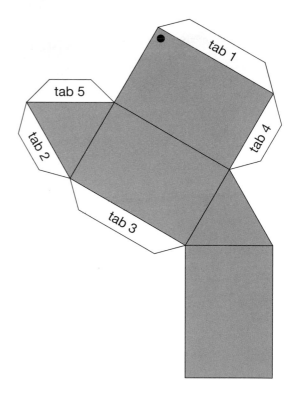

2 *2001 Paper 1*

The diagram shows a box. Draw the net for the box on a square grid.

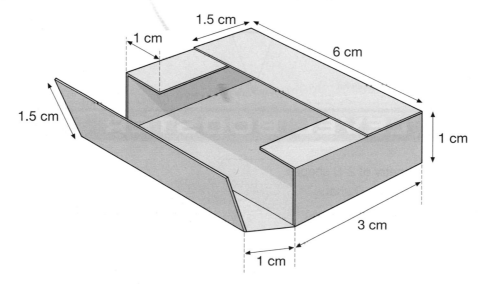

a   Any quadrilateral can be split into 2 triangles.

Explain how you know that the angles inside a quadrilateral add up to 360°.

b   What do the angles inside a pentagon add up to?

c   What do the angles inside a heptagon (7-sided shape) add up to?

Show your working.

Index

William Collins' dream of knowledge for all began with the publication of his first book in 1819. A self-educated mill worker, he not only enriched millions of lives, but also founded a flourishing publishing house. Today, staying true to this spirit, Collins books are packed with inspiration, innovation and practical expertise. They place you at the centre of a world of possibility and give you exactly what you need to explore it.

Collins. Freedom to teach.

Published by Collins
An imprint of HarperCollins*Publishers*
77–85 Fulham Palace Road
Hammersmith
London
W6 8JB

Browse the complete Collins catalogue at
www.collinseducation.com

© HarperCollins*Publishers* Limited 2008

10 9 8 7 6 5 4 3 2

ISBN 978-0-00-726610-4

Keith Gordon, Kevin Evans, Brian Speed and Trevor Senior assert their moral rights to be identified as the authors of this work.

British Library Cataloguing in Publication Data
A Catalogue record for this publication is available from the British Library.

Commissioned by Melanie Hoffman and Katie Sergeant
Project management by Priya Govindan
Edited by Karen Westall
Indexed by Michael Forder
Proofread by Amanda Dickson
Design and typesetting by Jordan Publishing Design
Covers by Oculus Design and Communications
Functional maths spreads and covers management by Laura Deacon
Illustrations by Nigel Jordan and Tony Wilkins
Printed and bound by Rotolito Lombarda, Italy
Production by Simon Moore

Acknowledgments
The publishers thank the Qualifications and Curriculum Authority for granting permission to reproduce questions from past National Curriculum Test papers for Key Stage 3 Maths.

The publishers wish to thank the following for permission to reproduce photographs:

p.14–15 (main image) © Jon Hicks / Corbis, p.46–47 (main image) © Van Hilversum / Alamy, p.46 (football image) © istockphoto.com, p.76–77 (main image) © istockphoto.com, p.76 (inset image) © istockphoto.com, p.88–89 (main image) © Ted Levine / zefa / Corbis, p.88–89 (inset images) © istockphoto.com, p.110–111 (main image) © Jeff Morgan food and drink / Alamy, p. 110–111 (all inset images) © istockphoto.com, p.128–129 (main image) © Science Photo Library, p. 128–129 (all inset images) © istockphoto.com, p.160–161 (main image) © Stephen Vowles / Alamy, p.170–171 (main image) © Sean Justice / Corbis, p.186–187 (all images) © istockphoto.com, p.212–213 (main and inset images) © istockphoto.com

Every effort has been made to trace copyright holders and to obtain their permission for the use of copyright material. The authors and publishers will gladly receive any information enabling them to rectify any error or omission at the first opportunity.

Mixed Sources
Product group from well-managed forests and other controlled sources
www.fsc.org Cert no. SW-COC-1806
© 1996 Forest Stewardship Council

FSC is a non-profit international organisation established to promote the responsible management of the world's forests. Products carrying the FSC label are independently certified to assure consumers that they come from forests that are managed to meet the social, economic and ecological needs of present and future generations.

Find out more about HarperCollins and the environment at
www.harpercollins.co.uk/green